SCHOOL CONNECTEDNESS FOR STUDENTS WITH DISABILITIES

School Connectedness for Students with Disabilities: From Theory to Evidence-based Practice focuses on the importance of school connectedness for students with disabilities, and presents ways in which this sense of connectedness can be fostered. Written from a holistic perspective, it embraces a variety of approaches, strategies and interventions rooted in evidence-based theory and practice, and examines them not only in regard to the student with a disability, but also school leaders, teachers, families and community members.

The book describes and defines the concept of school connectedness, provides the reader with a theoretical framework from which to examine connectedness and explores connectedness from the lens of each of its components. It discusses the importance of assessing school connectedness in order to make data-based intervention decisions, as well as unpacking the components of student engagement, school climate, bonding and attachment. Several school-wide and leadership approaches that foster school connectedness are presented, as are ways to involve families. All of these are discussed through the lens of disability, in order to acknowledge the characteristics of disability that affect student levels of school connectedness.

School connectedness has become a priority for many schools and educators internationally. Research demonstrates the importance of connectedness as a protective factor, and its impact on the health behaviour, social, emotional and academic outcomes of young people. Grounded in theory and relevant to practice, this is essential reading for anyone interested in improving the school connectedness of students with different disabilities across the lifespan.

Therese M. Cumming is an Associate Professor in Special Education in the School of Education at UNSW Sydney. Her publications include an edited book (*Sustaining Mobile Learning: Theory, research, and practice*, Routledge 2016), a co-authored book (*Lifespan Transitions for Individuals with Disabilities: A holistic perspective*, Routledge

2016), book chapters, journal articles and international conference papers. She also has many years of experience as a special educator.

Robbie J. Marsh is an Assistant Professor in Special Education at Mercer University. His research interests include: students with emotional and behavioural disorders and autism, access to mental health services and applied behaviour analysis.

Kyle Higgins is a Professor of Special Education in the Department of Educational & Clinical Studies at the University of Nevada Las Vegas. Her research interests focus on the use of technology and other evidence-based practices with students with disabilities to foster their inclusion in academic and non-academic settings.

SCHOOL CONNECTEDNESS FOR STUDENTS WITH DISABILITIES

From Theory to Evidence-based Practice

Therese M. Cumming, Robbie J. Marsh and Kyle Higgins

Routledge
Taylor & Francis Group

LONDON AND NEW YORK

First published 2018
by Routledge
2 Park Square, Milton Park, Abingdon, Oxon OX14 4RN

and by Routledge
711 Third Avenue, New York, NY 10017

Routledge is an imprint of the Taylor & Francis Group, an informa business

© 2018 Therese M. Cumming, Robbie J. Marsh and Kyle Higgins

British Library Cataloguing in Publication Data
A catalogue record for this book is available from the British Library

Library of Congress Cataloging in Publication Data
Names: Cumming, Therese M., author. | Marsh, Robbie J., author. | Higgins, Kyle, author.
Title: School connectedness for students with disabilities : from theory to evidence-based practice / Therese M. Cumming, Robbie J. Marsh and Kyle Higgins.
Description: Abingdon, Oxon ; New York, NY : Routledge, 2017. | Includes bibliographical references.
Identifiers: LCCN 2017007984 | ISBN 9781138081338 (hardback) | ISBN 9781138081352 (pbk.) | ISBN 9781315112930 (ebook)
Subjects: LCSH: Children with disabilities--Education. | School environment. | Attachment behavior in children. | Special education. | Inclusive education.
Classification: LCC LC4015 .C88 2017 | DDC 371.9--dc23
LC record available at https://lccn.loc.gov/2017007984

ISBN: 978-1-138-08133-8 (hbk)
ISBN: 978-1-138-08135-2 (pbk)
ISBN: 978-1-315-11293-0 (ebk)

Typeset in Bembo
by Taylor & Francis Books

We would like to dedicate this book to our family and friends who have understood our dedication to improving the lives of young people with disabilities, and supported us in our various endeavours in that direction.

Therese would like to especially thank Jim Cumming and Emily Smedley for their love, never ending belief in her and support.

Robbie would like to thank Jasmine Ringo, Robert Marsh and Susan Marsh for their love, support and endless patience.

This book would not have been possible without all of you.

CONTENTS

ILLUSTRATIONS

Figure

Tables

ABOUT THE AUTHORS

Therese M. Cumming is an Associate Professor in Special Education in the School of Education at UNSW Sydney. She has conducted special education research projects in both the USA and Australia. She has authored and co-authored numerous publications, including books, book chapters and journal articles in the areas of behavioural support, mobile technology, social skills instruction and inclusive research. Prior to her university and research work, Therese had 18 years' teaching experience in mainstream, special and mental health settings. Her ongoing research interests come under the umbrella of transition and include the use of technology to support students and families, positive behavioural interventions and supports, and inclusive education across the lifespan.

Robbie J. Marsh is an Assistant Professor in Special Education at Mercer University. He has authored and co-authored articles in the areas of behaviour support, mental health service access, mental health service policy and school connectedness. Prior to his work in higher education, he was the head of professional development and behavioural consultation for Miley Achievement Centre, a specialised school for students with emotional and behavioural disorders and high functioning autism, in the Clark County School District, Las Vegas, NV, USA. Robbie has eight years of teaching experience with students with disabilities on comprehensive campuses, specialised campuses and in residential mental health treatment facilities. His research interests include school connectedness of students with disabilities, in particular students with emotional and behavioural disorders, assessment development, student and teacher characteristics that contribute to school connectedness and the identification and service acquisition of students with mental health issues.

Kyle Higgins is a Professor of Special Education in the Department of Educational & Clinical Studies at the University of Nevada Las Vegas. She has worked in higher education for 29 years. Her research interests focus on the use of technology and other evidence-based practices with students with disabilities to foster their inclusion in academic and non-academic settings. To this end, she has created digital basal readers, designed a software evaluation tool to evaluate software for use with students with disabilities, and explored the use of social media with students with emotional behavioural disorders. She is past co-editor of the *Journal of Special Education Technology* (published by the Technology and Media Division of the Council for Exceptional Children) and the current co-editor of *Intervention in School and Clinic* (published by SAGE and the Hammill Institute on Disabilities). She is currently the co-project director on a federally funded project and just recently completed work on three federally funded projects in the USA.

FOREWORD

School Connectedness for Students with Disabilities: From Theory to Evidence-based Practice focuses on the importance of school connectedness for students with disabilities, and presents ways in which this sense of connectedness can be fostered. We label the book's perspective 'holistic', because it embraces a variety of approaches, strategies and interventions, which are rooted in evidence-based theory and practice, and these are examined not only in regard to the student with a disability, but also school leaders, teachers, families and community members.

The chapters contained within describe and define the concept of school connectedness, provide the reader with a theoretical framework from which to examine connectedness, and then examine connectedness from the lens of each of its components. We discuss the importance of assessing school connectedness in order to make data-based intervention decisions, as well as unpacking the components of student engagement, school climate, bonding and attachment. Several school-wide and leadership approaches that foster school connectedness are presented, as are ways to involve families. All of these are discussed from a lens of disability, in order to acknowledge the characteristics of disability that affect student levels of school connectedness.

School connectedness has become a priority for many schools and educators internationally. Research demonstrates the importance of connectedness as a protective factor, and its impact on the health behaviour, social, emotional and academic outcomes of young people. With this book, we endeavour to provide readers with this information, as well as a holistic view of how to improve the school connectedness of students with different disabilities across the lifespan.

ACKNOWLEDGEMENTS

This publication would not have been possible without the contributions of universities, researchers, teachers, families and most importantly, students with disabilities. We would like to thank all of the students with disabilities and their families, teachers and support staff members that we worked with, and those who have participated in our research studies throughout the years. Their experiences inspired us to write this book and to continue our efforts in promoting dialogue and eliciting change to improve the education and life experiences of those with disabilities.

1

INTRODUCTION

The idea that students benefit from a 'connection' to their school when they believe that teachers, students and administrators on their school campus care about them and their learning is central to the concept of school connectedness. This 'connection' has been studied in one form or another for more than three decades in the fields of psychology, education and sociology, and results have shown that students' beliefs about the extent to which adults care about their learning and overall well-being are central to academic success and emotional well-being. This variety of disciplines studying school connectedness has caused a general lack of agreement regarding its terminology and definition (Blum, 2005a). Terms such as school attachment, school bonding, school climate and school engagement have been used, but the authors of this proposed volume consider each of these to be a unique feature and one of the principal components of school connectedness. Current definitions of school connectedness focus on the extent to which a student feels that adults and peers whom are present in their academic environment care about them as individuals, their academic success and their overall well-being (Blum, 2005b; CDC, 2009).

Today's students have more complex needs than ever before, and the old frameworks of schooling no longer adequately serve their developmental needs (McLaughlin & Gray, 2015). High-stakes testing and accountability measures have placed the focus on students firmly in the area of academic achievement. This has been to the detriment of other areas that are crucial to adolescent development, such as relationships. School connectedness is a holistic construct, as it recognises that everything in a child's life is connected, and these connections have a strong impact on development (McLaughlin & Gray, 2015). Overall, school connectedness is about promoting protective factors and minimising risk factors in order to improve the quality of life and outcomes of young people (DASH-CDC, 2009).

Individual protective factors that have been found to protect young people against engagement in adverse behaviours include: school connectedness, parent-family connectedness, high parental expectations for academic achievement and the adolescent's level of involvement in religious activities and perceived importance of religion and prayer. School connectedness has been found to be the strongest protective factor for young people to decrease substance misuse, truancy, early sexual experience, violence, drinking, and driving without wearing a seatbelt (Resnick et al., 1997). It also has been found to be a protective factor against emotional distress, eating disorders and suicidal ideation and attempts (Resnick et al., 1997). A strong relationship has also been demonstrated between school connectedness and educational outcomes such as school attendance, school retention, and higher grades and test scores (Klem & Connell, 2004). The DASH-CDC report (2009) identified adult support, positive peer groups, commitment to education and school environment as four factors that can increase school connectedness.

Foundations of school connectedness

Scholars in the fields of psychology and educational psychology first explored the concept of school connectedness. They conducted theoretical explorations of the school environment in order to gain a better understanding of some of the problems experienced by adolescents such as: delinquency, early onset of sexual activity, violence and substance abuse (Bergin & Bergin, 2009; Kennedy & Kennedy, 2004). They determined that three major theories were foundational to school connectedness: (a) attachment theory, (b) social control theory and (c) the social development model (Chapman, Buckley, Sheehan & Shochet, 2013).

Attachment theory maintains that strong emotional and physical attachment to at least one primary caregiver is critical to a child's development, and affects future relationships (e.g., child/teacher, child/peers) (Ainsworth, 1979). These attachments are crucial in making the child feel secure and developing resilience (Bergin & Bergin, 2009). School bonding, which emphasises the bonds fostered between teachers and students, was developed from attachment theory (Chapman et al., 2013; Bergin & Bergin, 2009). Relationships between teachers and students have been shown to be of the utmost importance, as they have been shown to significantly impact student outcomes, health-risk behaviour and student engagement (Blum, 2005a; Libbey, 2004).

Proponents of social control theory theorise that the greater the bond an adolescent forms with parents, peers and school, the less likely the adolescent will engage in risk behaviours and become delinquent (Hirschi, 1969). Social control theory underpinned the development of both school bonding and school attachment, which emphasise the bond between the adolescent and school. While school bonding pertains to rules and the formation of relationships at school, school attachment focuses on the development of relationships and student satisfaction with school (Libbey, 2004).

The social development model suggests that adolescents learn pro-social or antisocial behaviours from their social environments (Bandura, 1997; Catalano, Haggerty, Oesterle, Fleming & Hawkins, 2004; Chapman et al., 2013). This highlights the importance of bonding, as when young people experience low levels of bonding it may result in antisocial behaviour. School bonding and school climate are based on the social development model.

The field of sociology went beyond the field of psychology and attempted to understand the levels of connectedness experienced by diverse groups. Sociologists focused on school climate, bonding and connectedness when studying children/ youth. School climate focuses on the environment, and how safe and welcoming it is (Booren, Handy & Power, 2011). School bonding evolved from the social control theory and emphasises the level of student involvement in relation to mis-behaviour and victimisation among adolescents (Peguero, Ovink & Ling, 2016; Popp & Peguero, 2012). The sociological goal of school connectedness is to iden-tify risk factors related to health risk behaviours and mental health issues, and differences among gender, ethnic and marginalised groups (Biag, 2014; Booth & Gerard, 2014).

The field of education studies school connectedness in order to design school-wide programming to enhance positive outcomes for students. The focus here is on fostering positive relationships among students, teachers and staff and developing positive school environments (DASH-CDC, 2009). Educators are concerned with school engagement, or how a student participates in academic and school related activities and how the student feels about school based on its social context.

Through the theoretical underpinnings and research of several disciplines, school connectedness has developed into a comprehensive concept that provides a multi-faceted framework for intervention to meet the complex needs of today's young people. These theoretical underpinnings are explored in more depth in Chapter 2.

School connectedness, as explored in this volume, incorporates additional social and emotional components related to overall student outcomes and is composed of four domains: (a) school bonding, (b) school attachment, (c) school engagement and (d) school climate (Bergin & Bergin, 2009; Blum, 2005a; Chapman et al., 2013; Cunningham, 2007; Libbey, 2004). These are well aligned with the com-ponents of connectedness suggested by the DASH-CDC (2009) listed in the previous section. This alignment is explored further in Chapter 2.

Much of the recent research on school connectedness has emerged in the ado-lescent health literature (Blum, 2005b; DASH-CDC, 2009; McNeely, Nonne-maker, & Blum, 2002; McNeely & Falci, 2004). This wide body of research has demonstrated that school connectedness is an important factor in reducing the likelihood that students will engage in behaviours that may compromise their well-being and health (McLaughlin & Clarke, 2010). Additionally, researchers have linked school connectedness to an increase in student academic success (Blum & Libbey, 2004). This is imperative to students with disabilities, many of whom have difficulties in both of these areas.

Importance of school connectedness for students with disabilities

Studies evaluating school connectedness as an intervention have largely been conducted with students in the general education environment (Catalano et al., 2004; Chapman et al., 2013), with little research focused on the overall levels of school connectedness for students with disabilities. Many of these students engage in misbehaviour, and traditional discipline policies, such as suspension and expulsion, can be exclusionary, which negatively affects the relationship between these students and their peers, teachers and administrators (Evans & Lester, 2012; Rivkin, 2009). This can adversely impact the school connectedness of this vulnerable population, for whom this sense of connectedness is of the utmost importance, as they often experience isolation and rejection when attempting to integrate within the school environment and beyond.

Due to the inherent characteristics of their disabilities, students with disabilities often experience problems creating and maintaining relationships with their teachers and peers and developing educational commitment. While the importance of relationships and behaviour has been much discussed in the literature, very little research addresses their use as part of a comprehensive programme of intervention. At no life stage are these relationships more important than in adolescence, a time of change and vulnerability for all young people, but possibly even more challenging for students with disabilities, who experience heightened vulnerability compared to their typically developing peers (Al-Yagon, 2016). Reasons for this, along with suggestions for intervention are explored further in Chapter 5.

Conclusion

School connectedness is a preventative approach that holistically addresses issues related to the school-to-prison pipeline, school retention, academic achievement, bullying and engagement in health-risk behaviour (Blum & Libbey, 2004; Shippen, Patterson, Green & Smitherman, 2012). This comprehensive framework of interventions targets the school connectedness levels of students with disabilities, and has the potential to address their social, emotional and academic needs as well as create safe learning environments (McLaughlin & Clarke, 2010). This book's focus is on the importance of school connectedness for students with disabilities, and ways in which this sense of connectedness can be fostered are at the core of this discussion.

Much intervention research in the area of school connectedness involves strategies designed to foster positive student relationships with teachers as well as their peers (Anderson-Butcher, 2010; Shippen et al., 2012). These interventions include the development of programs that: (a) seek to promote family involvement, (b) aim to utilise culturally responsive pedagogy, (c) work to integrate community leaders into school life and (d) focus on bullying prevention (Anderson-Butcher, 2010; O'Brennan, Waasdorp & Bradshaw, 2014; Toshalis, 2015). The chapters contained in this book provide an in-depth look at each of these different types of interventions, the research that supports their use and their effective implementation. The overall goal is to put forward an integrated and holistic approach to school connectedness.

2

THE SCHOOL CONNECTEDNESS PARADIGM

A theoretical perspective

School connectedness is a multifaceted framework for intervention that has emerged in the literature, spanning multiple fields of research, regarding adolescent health and well-being (Blum, 2005a; Blum & Libbey, 2004; DASH-CDC, 2009; Klem & Connell, 2004; McNeely et al., 2002; McNeely & Falci, 2004; Resnick et al., 1997). As a framework, school connectedness was developed from theories deeply rooted in the fields of psychology and sociology. Attachment theory, social control theory and the social development model all outline specific social phenomena experienced by individuals from birth to early adulthood (Ainsworth & Bowlby, 1991; Catalano & Hawkins, 1996; Hirschi, 1969). Each of these theories were developed to explain the ways in which children and adolescents develop and maintain interpersonal relationships as well as navigate their social environments, and offer insight as to how best to improve student academic and behavioural outcomes.

This chapter will examine the theoretical framework used to develop the construct of school connectedness. Each of the three major theories (i.e., attachment theory, social control theory, social development model) that contributed to the development of the school connectedness construct will be discussed as well as the role these theories play in differing fields of research. The chapter will conclude with a brief discussion of the domains of school connectedness developed from the four major fields of research and will act as a foundational discussion for the chapters that follow.

Attachment theory

Attachment theory refers to an emotional bond that is developed by a child during infancy (Bowlby, 2007). The theory is predicated on the works of John Bowlby and Mary Ainsworth, who helped to develop the theory by observing interactions between mothers and their infants (Ainsworth & Bowlby, 1991; Shaver, Collins &

Clark, 1996). Secure infant attachment is developed through proximity of a primary caregiver, typically the mother, who acts as a base of security for an infant to explore their environment (Ainsworth & Bowlby, 1991; Bowlby, J. 1982; Bowlby, R. 2007; Shaver et al., 1996). This secure attachment is represented by the caregiver's ability to effectively comfort the infant when they become frightened or hurt (Bowlby, 2007). Although the primary caregiver is the primary attachment figure early in an infant's life, secondary attachment figures, individuals who are a regular part of the infant's life (e.g., neighbour, friend, grandparent), are also able to comfort the infant in times of distress (Bowlby, 2007). These attachments are carried on through the child's life, and are represented by the development of predictable, safe and affectionate bonds created through adulthood (Bowlby, 2007; Reuther, 2014; Shaver et al., 1996).

Depending on the predictability of the behaviour of the primary or secondary caregivers, infants may develop secure or insecure attachment bonds (Bowlby, 1982; Shaver et al., 1996). Secure attachments are a result of the infant's ability to consistently access the primary caregiver, typically through crying, when in distress. This results in the infant's willingness to explore their environment more frequently as well as easier comforting by the caregiver when the infant becomes distressed (Ainsworth & Bowlby, 1991; van Rosmalen, van der Horst & van der Veer, 2016; Shaver et al., 1996). Insecure attachments can consist of either anxious-ambivalent attachments or avoidant attachments. Anxious-ambivalent attachments are a result of inconsistent access to the primary caregiver resulting in crying when separated from the primary caregiver and the inability for the caregiver to comfort them once reunited (Ainsworth & Bowlby, 1991; van Rosmalen et al., 2016; Shaver et al., 1996). Avoidant attachment is the result of unresponsive or unavailable caregivers (Shaver et al. 1996). Avoidant infants do not cry when separated from their primary caregiver and avoid the primary caregiver once reunited (Ainsworth & Bowlby, 1991). These types of early attachments affect the child's ability to form bonds and extend through the course of their life with more secure bonds creating better future outcomes (Bergin & Bergin, 2009; Chapman et al., 2013).

The creation of bonds to more than three secure attachment figures is paramount to promote a child's resilience and mental health (Bowlby, 2007; Chapman et al., 2013). Children develop, according to Bowlby, working models of attachment predicated on the actions of different individuals (Bowlby, 1982; Shaver et al., 1996). The type of attachment created, secure or insecure, is dependent on the communication ability of each individual. Secure attachments are formed with individuals who are open, honest, predictable and easy to understand, whereas insecure attachments are formed with individuals who are closed off, unpredictable, passive, unresponsive and difficult to understand (Bretherton, 1990; Shaver et al., 1996).

Ultimately, early interactions between the primary caregiver and the infant create an initial framework by which the child uses to develop relationships over the course of his or her lifetime (Reuther, 2014; van Rosmalen et al., 2016). This framework is expanded and revised through experiences with other secondary attachment figures throughout the child's lifetime (Ainsworth & Bowlby, 1991; Bowlby, 2007; Reuther, 2014). An individual's behaviours are a result of those attachments, secure or insecure, and are developed and maintained by peer groups, occupational choices, romantic partners and religious and cultural influences (Reuther, 2014). These sociocultural practices and experiences model and shape how individuals develop and maintain interpersonal relationships.

Social control theory

While attachment theory focuses primarily on the development of interpersonal relationships beginning with the early interactions of a child's life, social control theory focuses on behaviour during adolescence. Originally developed by Hirschi (1969), social control theory was developed as a means of explaining delinquent behaviour in adolescents. Hirschi (1969) theorised that the development and maintenance of social bonds in adolescence is predicated on conformity to societal norms and values (Johnson, 1984). These bonds exist in four domains: (a) attachment, (b) commitment, (c) involvement and (d) belief (Hirschi, 1969; Johnson, 1984; Wiatrowski, Griswold & Roberts, 1981). The strength of each of these bonds predicts an adolescent's likelihood to engage in delinquent behaviour (Hirschi, 1969; Johnson, 1984).

Similar to Bowlby and Ainsworth's definition (1991), attachment refers to the extent an adolescent is able to create and maintain interpersonal relationships (Alston, Harley & Lenhoff, 1995; Bowman, Krohn, Gibson & Stogner, 2012). An adolescent's ability to develop interpersonal relationships may be shaped by family members, community members or peers (Wiatrowski et al., 1981). Adolescents with strong attachments to their family, community, schools and peers are presumed to be less likely to violate the values upheld by these individuals or institutions (Alston et al., 1995; Hirschi, 1969). Conversely, adolescents with weak social attachments are viewed as unconcerned about the values of these social groups and are therefore more likely to engage in behaviour that violates those values (Alston et al., 1995; Hirschi, 1969). Ultimately, the attachment domain is primarily concerned with whether or not an adolescent is concerned about developing and maintaining positive social bonds with the individuals and institutions in their lives (Johnson, 1984).

Commitment refers to the amount of time an adolescent invests in social activities and institutions (e.g., school, church) and their aspirations for the future (Alston et al., 1995; Johnson, 1984; Wiatrowski et al., 1981). Hirschi (1969) proposed that there is an association to the amount of time and effort an individual invests in activities related to personal goals (e.g., going to college). The more invested the individual, the less likely they are to engage in behaviour that would prohibit them from achieving their goals (Alston et al., 1995; Wiatrowski et al., 1981). Adolescents who have not made a heavy investment towards their future and lack defined goals for the future are therefore less inhibited by goal-oriented behaviour and are more likely to engage in delinquent behaviour (Hirschi, 1969).

While commitment refers to the goals and investing time towards achieving those goals, involvement refers to the specific behaviours performed by an adolescent in order to achieve those goals. The more time an adolescent is engaged in completing school work, participating in after-school activities, helping around the house, engaging in family-structured activities, employment or other community-organised endeavours, the less time there is available to engage in delinquent behaviour (Alston et al., 1995; Hirschi, 1969; Johnson, 1984). Individuals who are less involved in structured activities, therefore have more free time available and are more likely to engage in delinquent behaviour (Alston et al., 1995; Hirschi, 1969). Time spent engaging in school-related activities is viewed as a precursor for achieving educational goals, which in turn increases the opportunity to obtain meaningful employment (Wiatrowski et al., 1981).

The final domain of social control theory is belief. Belief refers to the extent an individual believes in the moral validity of shared social values and norms (Alston et al., 1995; Hirschi, 1969; Wiatrowski et al., 1981). Hirschi (1969) proposed that individuals who hold true the beliefs and values of society are less likely to engage in behaviour that deviates from them. Unfortunately, beliefs and values differ across cultural and ethnic norms and can get complicated and confusing (Alston et al., 1995). For example, the belief systems held by Americans regarding legal medically prescribed narcotics, alcohol consumption, sexual activity and marijuana use are drastically different and influenced by age, peer groups, sociocultural norms and socioeconomic status (Alston et al., 1995; Chapman et al., 2013). Regardless, Hirschi (1969) proposed that as belief in guidelines decreases, the likelihood for engaging in delinquent behaviour increases.

While social control theory was originally developed to explain delinquency in adolescents, it offers something more in addressing a variety of variables that influence behaviour. Adolescence is a period of great physiological change and is accompanied by changing social dynamics within the school, home and community environments (Blum, 2005a; Merikangas et al., 2010). As adolescents socialise with different peer groups, have experiences with different adults in their lives (e.g., mentors, teachers, community leaders), develop goals for the future, and participate in structured activities, their behaviours will begin to match the values and belief systems of those they associate (Alston et al., 1995; Bandura, 1979; Blum, 2005a; Hirschi, 1969; Wiatrowski, 1981).

Social development model

The social development model is a reconceptualisation of the social control theory. Catalano and Hawkins (1996) extended the social control theory to include components of self-control theory, social learning theory and differential association theory (Bandura, 1979; Catalano, Haggerty, Oesterle, Fleming & Hawkins, 2004; Gottfredson & Hirschi, 1990; Matsueda, 1988). Catalano and Hawkins (1996) suggested that an individual's ability to create and maintain pro-social bonds depends on levels of attachment and commitment; however involvement is viewed a part of this process, not a separate entity, and belief is the outcome of bonds that have been created by the individual (Catalano et al., 2004).

Self-control theory refers to an individual's ability to defer gratification, with those individuals who lack self-control more likely to engage in behaviour that results in immediate gratification (Gottfredson & Hirschi, 1990; Sorenson & Brownfield, 1995). In conjunction with social control theory, individuals with low self-control will struggle with the involvement domain, as engaging in behaviours in order to pursue and ultimate goal requires significant delays in gratification (Hirschi, 1969; Chapman et al., 2013). Social development model takes into account that adolescents may struggle to delay gratification and suggests that adolescents need to be taught the skills necessary for effective goal-setting and require opportunities to practise these skills over time as well as receive reinforcement from their involvement behaviour (Catalano & Hawkins, 1996; Catalano et al., 2004; Chapman et al., 2013).

Social learning theory centres on the ability of an individual to perform behaviours in conjunction with social standards and self-reflect on the effectiveness of the performance of those behaviours (Bandura, 1979). Bandura (1979) proposed that goal-directed behaviours are guided by an individual's ability to predict the outcome of performing certain behaviours, which is shaped by imitation and a history of reinforcement, to achieve certain goals and avoid punishment (Grusec, 1992). Social development model draws upon the principles of social learning theory by emphasising the development of pro-social bonds with positive peer groups and the skills necessary for developing those bonds (Catalano & Hawkins, 1996; Catalano et al., 2004; Chapman et al., 2013).

Similar to the social learning theory, differential association theory is concerned with delinquent behaviour related to social norms of groups (e.g., peer groups, community groups, school groups) and the individual experiences adolescents have as members of different groups (Matsueda, 1988; Sutherland, 1973). An individual develops their stance on rule following based on the groups they are associated with, and as they encounter more stringent beliefs against delinquent behaviour or more favourable beliefs towards delinquent behaviour, they are likely to adjust their behaviour towards the prevailing beliefs of the groups with which they belong (Matsueda, 1988). Social development model takes these principles into account, along with the principles of social learning theory, and further emphasises the development of adolescent pro-social bonds to positive peer groups as well as development of parent/family pro-social bonds (Catalano & Hawkins, 1996; Catalano et al., 2004).

Social development model, although built on the foundation of social control theory, offers a more comprehensive view of the development of pro-social bonds and the variables that play a part in that development. While emphasising the importance of attachment and commitment, explained through the social control theory, the role of involvement is viewed as a series of opportunities to interact with various social groups and apply the skills necessary to be a functioning member of those groups (Catalano & Hawkins, 1996; Catalano et al., 2004; Chapman et al., 2013). Belief in social norms is a by-product of an adolescent's successful membership in positive groups (e.g., peer, community, school) (Catalano et al., 2004). Social development model extends the thought of bonds to include important socialising units of children/youth as playing a major role in the development of pro-social or antisocial behaviours (Catalano et al., 2004). A young person will engage in behaviour consistent with the behaviours and values held by peers, family, school and community (Bandura, 1979; Catalano & Hawkins, 1996; Catalano et al., 2004; Chapman et al., 2013; Matsueda, 1988).

School connectedness by discipline

Currently, there is a variety of terms used to describe various aspects of school connectedness. Research in this area spans the fields of educational psychology, psychology, sociology, health sciences and education (Blum, 2005a). Because school connectedness is a term synonymous with school attachment, school bonding, school climate and school engagement, the term itself has not been defined clearly and is used synonymously these fields of research (Blum, 2005a; Libbey, 2004). The most comprehensive definition of school connectedness, outlined by the field of health sciences, focuses on the extent to which a student feels that adults and peers in their academic environment care about them as individuals, their academic success and their overall well-being (Blum, 2005a; DASH-CDC, 2009). To better understand school connectedness as a construct, the contributions and research conducted in each field of study should be examined.

Field of psychology / educational psychology

The foundations of school connectedness were first discussed in the field of psychology. Educational psychologists then applied psychological theories to the educational environment to better understand adolescent engagement in delinquency, sexuality, violence and substance abuse (Bergin & Bergin, 2009; Chapman et al., 2013; Kennedy & Kennedy, 2004; Target, Fonagy & Shmueli-Goetz, 2003). Three major theories foundational to school connectedness (attachment theory, social control theory and the social development model) were used as a basis to understand the educational environment using the terms school attachment and school bonding (Chapman et al., 2013).

Attachment theory maintains that early bonding between a parent and child extends to other relationships (e.g., child/teacher, child/peers, child/extended family) (Ainsworth, 1979; Ainsworth & Bowlby, 1991). Secure attachments can aid in the development of personal security and resilience while insecure attachments hinder a sense of personal security and social development (Bergin & Bergin, 2009). The concept of school bonding, developed from attachment theory, links the bonds created between teachers and students (Bergin & Bergin, 2009; Chapman et al., 2013; Kennedy & Kennedy, 2004). Secure bonds between teachers and students have been shown to improve student outcomes, reduce engagement in health-risk behaviour and increase student engagement (Anderson,

Christenson, Sinclair & Lehr, 2004; Blum, 2005a; Libbey, 2004; McNeely & Falci, 2004).

Social control theory also focuses on the concept of bonding. It suggests that the greater the bond between an adolescent and people or institutions, the less likely the adolescent will engage in delinquent behaviour, which would violate the values and beliefs of those people or institutions (Hirschi, 1969). These bonds extend to individual relationships with parents and peers as well as bonds with school and community institutions (Catalano et al., 2004; Chapman et al., 2013; Hirschi, 1969). School bonding and school attachment both evolved from social control theory, which extended the notion of bonding from individuals to institutions. School bonding refers to involvement and belief in school rules, as well as the role the level of involvement and belief plays in the formation of interpersonal relationships on a school campus (Libbey, 2004). School attachment refers to the development of relationships on a school campus, including teacher and peer relationships, as well as an individual's overall satisfaction with school (Bearman & Moody, 2004; Libbey, 2004).

The social development model, developed from social learning theory, suggests that an adolescent's level of bonding to their social environment plays a role in engagement in either pro-social or antisocial behaviours (Bandura, 1997; Catalano et al., 2004; Chapman et al., 2013). Once a bond is developed, an adolescent will choose to engage in pro-social or antisocial behaviour depending on the norms, values, and environmental factors held by the group or institution with which the bond is held (Catalano et al., 2004). School bonding and school climate are core to the social development model. School bonding can be defined as the extent to which an adolescent is involved in school activities, including the amount of opportunities afforded to them to participate in school activities and the acquisition of skills necessary to be successful in school activities (Catalano & Hawkins, 1996). School climate refers to the norms and values of the school community (Blum & Libbey, 2004; Libbey, 2004). School climate is comprised of: (a) school discipline policies, (b) positive behavioural supports, (c) fairness of rules, (d) enforcement of rules and (e) the development of student–teacher relationships (Libbey, 2004).

Field of sociology

While the fields of psychology and educational psychology highlight the roles school bonding, attachment and climate play in adolescent social development, the field of sociology attempts to understand the school experiences of diverse groups. School climate and bonding are the predominate constructs in sociology related to children/youth. School climate focuses on student feelings and experiences in relation to the school environment, including instances of school violence and school safety practices (e.g., the extent to which students feel safe on campus) (Booren, Handy & Power, 2011; Gottfredson, Gottfredson, Payne & Gottfredson, 2005; Thapa, Cohen, Guffey & Higgins-D'Alessandro, 2013). School bonding focuses on the level of student involvement in relation to misbehaviour and victimisation among adolescents (Cunningham, 2007; Peguero, Ovink & Ling, 2016; Peguero, Popp, Latimore, Shekarkhar & Koo, 2011; Popp & Peguero, 2012). In the field of sociology, the goal of school connectedness research is the identification of certain experiences that may become risk factors for substance abuse, violence, sexuality, mental health issues and differences among gender and ethnic groups (Biag, 2014; Booth & Gerard, 2014; Chung-Do, Goesbert, Hamagani, Chang & Hishinuma, 2015; Dornbusch, Erickson, Laird & Wong, 2001; Loukas, Cance & Batanova, 2013; Ozer, Wolf & Kong, 2008).

Field of health science

Similar to the sociological perspective, research in the field of health science is concerned with further understanding school connectedness. In 1997, Resnick et al. called attention to the factors related to adolescent health and well-being. By analysing data from The National Longitudinal Study of Adolescent Health (Add Health), Resnick et al. (1997) examined the impact of three categories of characteristics: (a) family, (b) school and (c) individual on engagement in health-risk behaviour (e.g., emotional distress, violence towards self or others, substance abuse, sexual behaviour) (Add Health, 1995). As a result, they discovered that of all the characteristics examined, parent-family connectedness and school connectedness were the only two factors that provided protection for adolescents engaging in health-risk behaviour (Resnick et al., 1997). Furthermore, school connectedness was found to be protective against all of the health-risk behaviours examined (Resnick et al., 1997).

The results of the Resnick et al. (1997) study began a discussion concerning school connectedness that lasted into the early part of the 21st century. Researchers continued to examine the Add Health data set to analyse relationships between demographic variables and levels of school connectedness (Bearman & Burns, 1998; Bearman & Moody, 2004; McNeely & Falci, 2004; McNeely, Nonnemaker & Blum, 2002). The results of this research revealed that high levels of school connectedness are not only protective against engagement in health-risk behaviour but act as a predictor for positive school related outcomes (e.g., academic achievement, graduation) (Bearman & Moody, 2004; McNeely et al., 2002).

With these findings, the Center for Disease Control Division of Adolescent and School Health (DASH) convened researchers to compile the school connectedness research and write key recommendations for educators concerning development of levels of connectedness on school campuses (DASH-CDC, 2009). In 2004, the *Journal of School Health* commissioned six papers for a special school connectedness issue, which provided a compilation of current school connectedness research (Catalano et al., 2004; Blum & Libbey, 2004; Klem & Connel, 2004; Libbey; 2004; McNeely & Falci, 2004). Topics such as teacher–student relationships, school climate, academic achievement and school engagement, sense of belonging, school bonding and attachment, development of positive peer groups, and school environmental factors were included in the journal and were aggregated as a set of recommendations made to the CDC (Blum & Libbey, 2004; Catalano et al., 2004; CDC, 2009; Klem & Connell, 2004; McNeely & Falci, 2004).

Field of education

As a result of the CDC report, the field of education began to take notice of school connectedness as an important student outcome variable. School connectedness in the field of education is purposeful and directly related to the design of school-wide programming to enhance positive outcomes for individuals. This involves the creation of positive relationships among students, teachers and staff, levels of school engagement and the development of positive school environments (DASH-CDC, 2009; Farrington et al., 2012; Furlong, Whipple, St. Jean, Simental, Soliz & Punthuna, 2003; Jimerson, Campos & Greif, 2003).

School engagement refers to school-related behaviours involving: (a) participation in academic activities within the classroom, (b) participation in school-sponsored activities, (c) enjoyment of school activities and (d) beliefs and perceptions based on the social context of school (Furlong et al., 2003; Jimerson et al., 2003). School engagement research also is concerned with adolescent behaviours within the context of the class-room (e.g., turning in homework, completing class assignments, being organised, attending class, tardiness), beliefs and perceptions used to solve academic and social issues and develop solutions and social skills used to develop relationships with peers and adults (Farrington et al., 2012). Thus, school engagement is considered to be a major component required to build school connectedness (DASH-CDC, 2009).

The school connectedness construct

While school engagement provides the foundation for the academic and social facets of the school experience, school bonding and school attachment add to the construct by incorporating additional social and emotional components related to overall student outcomes (Blum, 2005a; DASH-CDC, 2009; Farrington et al., 2012; Newman, Lohman & Newman, 2007; O'Brennan, et al., 2014). According to the DASH-CDC report (2009), school connectedness is comprised of four components: (a) adult support, (b) positive peer group support, (c) commitment to education and (d) school environment. Adult support refers to the development of the student–teacher relationship, also referred to as school bonding and school attachment when incorporating psychological and sociological perspectives (Catalano et al., 2004; CDC, 2009; Chapman et al., 2013; Cunningham, 2007). Belonging to a positive peer group was also evolved from psychological and sociological works of school bonding and school attachment (DASH-CDC, 2009; Catalano et al., 2004; Chapman et al., 2013; Cunningham, 2007). Commitment to education was developed from the educational research regarding school engagement (DASH-CDC, 2009; Furlong et al., 2003; Jimerson et al., 2003). And, finally, the school environment, directly linked to the research conducted in the health sciences, refers to the overall climate of a school (Booren et al., 2011; DASH-CDC, 2009; Gottfredson et al., 2005; Thapa et al., 2013).

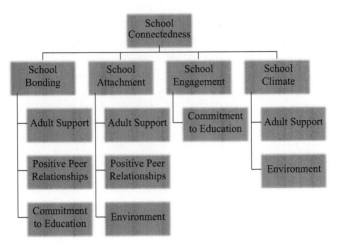

FIGURE 2.1 School connectedness and the accompanying four domains along with their relation to the four components of school connectedness outlined by the DASH-CDC report (2009).

Therefore, school connectedness is a comprehensive construct made up of four specific domains (i.e., school bonding, school attachment, school engagement, school climate), having both ties to the components of school connectedness outlined by the DASH-CDC report (2009) as well as the four major fields of research (see Figure 2.1).

The reality is that each domain of school connectedness plays an important role in contributing to a student's overall sense of school connectedness (Bergin & Bergin, 2009; Blum, 2005a; Booren et al., 2011; Catalano et al., 2004; CDC, 2009; Chapman et al., 2013; Cunningham, 2007; Furlong et al., 2003; Jimerson et al., 2003; Libbey, 2004; Thapa et al., 2013). As education shifts focus towards the comprehensive development of children and youth, school connectedness must be at the forefront of the conversation due to its relationship to the social, academic and psychological outcomes of students (Blum, 2005a; DASH-CDC, 2009; Libbey 2004; McNeely et al., 2002).

School bonding

School bonding refers to extent to which students are able to create and maintain relationships with adults and peers on their school campus (Ainsworth & Bowlby, 1991; Chapman et al., 2013; Hirschi, 1969). From these relationships, students adopt values held by the groups with which they belong and affects their level of commitment to school (Bandura, 1979; Catalano & Hawkins, 1996; Catalano et al., 2004; Matsueda, 1988). The development of school bonding is dependent on the level of adult support a student receives, positive peer relationships, and a commitment to education (Blum, 2005a). Each of these components builds on another in the development of positive, secure bonds with teachers, staff, and students present in the school environment (Ainsworth & Bowlby, 1991; Catalano & Hawkins, 1996; Catalano et al., 2004). Chapter 6 contains an in-depth discussion of school bonding, as well as ways to develop school bonding in students.

School attachment

School attachment refers to the view a student holds about the school experience (Libbey, 2004). This includes whether or not the students feel they are liked by adults and peers on campus, enjoy being at school and feel like contributing members to the school environment, which affects their level of involvement in school (Catalano et al., 2004; Hirschi, 1969). The development of school attachment is dependent on the level of adult support, positive peer relationships and environmental factors (Blum, 2005a). A student's level of school attachment is dependent on the amount of positive secure bonds they have created (Ainsworth & Bowlby, 1991; Bowlby, 2007; Shaver et al., 1996). In addition to the amount of secure bonds, the availability of activities, as well as the degree of opportunity to engage in those activities, further affects a student's level of school attachment (Blum, 2005a; Catalano et al., 2004). Chapter 6 contains an in-depth discussion of school attachment as well as ways to improve levels of school attachment in students.

School engagement

School engagement refers to the degree to which a student engages in school-related behaviours (Catalano et al., 2004; Farrington et al., 2012; Jimerson et al., 2003). School-related behaviour consists of regularly attending school, arriving to class on time, completing class work, completing homework, regularly turning in assignments and participating in classroom discussion and activities (Farrington et al., 2012; Jimerson et al., 2003). School engagement is the application of behaviours related to a student's level of involvement in school (Catalano et al., 2004). Students with higher levels of school engagement display higher levels of commitment to their education by frequently engaging in school-related behaviours in order to achieve their academic and post-secondary goals (Farrington et al., 2012; Gottfredson & Hirschi, 1990; Jimerson et al., 2003; Sorenson & Brownfield, 1995). A student's ability to defer gratification to achieve an ultimate goal will affect their level of school engagement (Catalano et al., 2004; Gottfredson & Hirschi, 1990; Sorenson & Brownfield, 1995). Chapter 7 contains an in-depth discussion of school engagement as well as ways to develop school-related skills in order to improve student levels of school engagement.

School climate

School climate refers to the extent a student feels safe in their school environment and the degree to which staff implement policies and interventions to promote engagement in pro-social behaviour (Vincent, Horner & Sugai, 2002; U.S. Department of Education, 2014). A student's reported level of school climate is dependent on the degree of adult support directed to the promotion of positive school behaviour, which affects the overall school environment as well as the degree to which students feel safe in that environment (McNeely et al., 2002; Vincent et al., 2002). Schools that promote overly harsh discipline policies for minor student infractions or employ teachers who struggle to effectively manage classroom behaviour unintentionally create unsafe learning environments that affect student levels of school climate (McNeely et al., 2002; Vincent et al., 2002). Chapter 3 contains an in-depth discussion of school climate as well as ways to build a positive school climate for students as well as staff.

Conclusion

The preceding discussion is intended to provide a theoretical understanding of the foundations of school connectedness. A thorough understanding of the foundations of school connectedness and their relation to differing fields of inquiry offer educators a comprehensive view of child/youth social development and the role it plays in their educational experiences. While some of these theories may seem dated and portray narrowed views of child/youth development, they have been extensively researched for many years in order to be honed and refined, and they offer possible explanations to student-related or school-related barriers that educators currently experience in regards to working with students with disabilities.

Students with disabilities may experience gaps in their social and emotional development that can affect their ability to effectively navigate the school environment (Chapman et al., 2013; Durlak, Weissberg, Dymnicki, Taylor & Schellinger, 2011; Gresham, 2002). These gaps affect their development of pro-social behaviours as well as school-related behaviours, which increases their risk of becoming disconnected from the school environment (Catalano et al., 2004; Chapman et al., 2013; Hawkins, Von Cleve & Catalano, 1991; Toshalis, 2015). Moving through the rest of the book, school connectedness, broken down into its four domains, will be discussed as a means for addressing issues related to the school experiences of students with disabilities, their families, and teachers and school staff working with students with disabilities.

3

SCHOOL CLIMATE AND ITS EFFECTS ON SCHOOL CONNECTEDNESS

School climate

School climate is a multidimensional construct that has been studied for over 100 years, with scientific study beginning in the 1950s (Gage, Larson, Sugai & Chafouleas, 2016; Zullig, Koopman, Patton & Ubbes, 2010). In the 1970s, researchers found that school climate was linked to the differences in outcomes between schools, and was the greatest indicator was how students felt about themselves at school (Zullig et al., 2010). Beginning in the 1990s and continuing today, researchers have attempted to link school climate to student achievement, aggression, bullying, crime, attachment, bonding, connectedness, engagement and alcohol and drug use (Zullig et al., 2010). Although there is a lack of consensus in the literature, policy and practice documents on the definition of school climate, there is general agreement on its importance in improving student academic outcomes and preventing social and behavioural difficulties (Gage et al., 2016).

Definitions

As stated above, there is no consensus in the literature when it comes to a standard definition of school climate. The definitions are similar in that most include the areas of relationships, instructional practices and the organisational structure of schools. For example, Cohen, McCabe, Michelli and Pickeral (2009) claim that school climate is the quality and character of school life, and is based on people's shared experiences including norms, goals, values, relationships, teaching and learning practices and organisational structures.

The National School Climate Center (NSCC) (2009) maintains that a positive school climate is the overall quality of school life, and involves norms, values and expectations that support social, emotional and physical safety, includes school community members who are engaged and respected, and strives for collaboration between students, families and educators to develop and work towards a shared school vision. The Council's vision of a positive school climate also includes educators who model and encourage positive attitudes towards learning. Lastly, all members of the school community should be active contributors to the operations of the school and care of its physical environment.

Coulston and Smith (2013) define school climate as "the holistic context of the life, vigour, and quality of the social connectedness, physical elements, and supportive practices that nurture inclusion and safeness" (p. 1). Gage et al. (2016) define school climate based on several previous definitions: "the shared beliefs, values, and attitudes that shape interactions between students, teachers, and administrators and set the parameters of acceptable behaviour and norms for the school" (p. 1). Perhaps the best way to come to a consensus on a working definition of school climate is to look at the domains of school climate suggested in the literature. Drilling the definition of school climate down to its domains provides a solid framework for the creation of a comprehensive, scientifically sound assessment that schools can use to evaluate their climate and plan for improvement (NSCC, 2009).

Domains

Although the number of school climate domains varies in the literature, researchers agree that school climate is shaped by at least four major areas: safety, relationships, academic outcomes and supports and the school's physical environment (Cohen et al., 2009). More recently, researchers have added other domains, specifically school connectedness, and subdomains that more precisely define the domains (Petrie, 2014; Zullig et al., 2010).

Safety

The term safety encompasses both physical and socio-emotional safety. Examples of school context that typically fall under this domain are order and discipline, crisis planning, attitudes about violence, respect for diversity, students' and adults' response towards bullying (Cohen et al., 2009). Students who perceived themselves safe in school reported higher level of satisfaction (Zullig et al., 2010; Zullig et al., 2011). Schools which have clearly communicated rules that are equally applicable to all students, follow shared problem solving strategies and maintain fair disciplinary practice are perceived to promote a positive student experience (Zullig et al., 2010; Zullig et al., 2011). Such order and discipline also enhances the predictability of the school environment as well as ensuring both physical and emotional safety (Cohen et al., 2009), resulting in positive student attitudes towards the schooling process.

Relationships

Relationships have been cited as one of the most important domains of school climate (Cohen et al., 2009; Petrie, 2014; Zullig et al., 2010; Zullig et al., 2011).

This includes student–peer relationships, as well as student–teacher relationships, helpfulness of staff and interpersonal relationships (Zullig et al., 2011). Petrie (2014) found that the strongest body of evidence to support the improvement of school climate was in the area of improving student–teacher relationships.

Students spend much of their time at school interacting with teachers during teaching-learning activities. Hence, a student's relationships with his or her teachers are considered to be very influential in regards to a positive school climate. Teachers are also viewed as the most significant providers of social support for students, in that they support and promote school connectedness, academic competence and self-esteem among students (DeSantis King, Huebner, Suldo & Valois, 2006). Positive student–teacher relationships contribute to positive school experiences across all grades, though the effect may vary between primary and secondary schooling (Kim & Kim, 2013). When students perceive that teachers are nurturing and supportive, they feel satisfied, engaged and are more likely to receive positive feedback in class, which further results in more school satisfaction (Ding & Hall, 2007). Danielsen, Samdal, Hetland and Wold (2009) claim that a teacher's warmth, care and individual attention helps students to feel more competent, and influences more positive classroom engagement and academic motivation.

Teachers may foster bonding between classmates and cultivate a learning community, where students experience feelings of acceptance and belonging to the classroom as well as school environment; this further leads to better adjustment and positive school experiences (Kim & Kim, 2013). Teachers also have the potential to reduce negative school experiences like peer victimisation, peer rejection and loneliness by addressing conflicts and bullying issues (Danielsen et al., 2009). Overall, positive student–teacher relationships provide students with multiple supports – academic, emotional and social, which have the potential to promote school as a place of meaning and worth.

Relationships among peers, classmates and friends have been another important influence over positive school climate (Baker, Dilly, Aupperlee & Patil, 2003; Danielsen et al., 2009; DeSantis King et al., 2006; Kim & Kim, 2013). Peer support for learning has been found to significantly affect students' school satisfaction and perception of school climate. Peer acceptance and friendship are also influential factors; students who feel accepted by their peers tend to be more attuned with the school environment (Danielsen et al., 2009). Osterman (2000) discovered that acceptance was more important than friendship in the context of school satisfaction; whereas friendship only indicates close bonding with some specific individual within the school community, peer acceptance indicates belonging to the school community.

Students who perceive classmates and peers as more supportive tend to experience less peer bullying and as a result they tend to like school more (Wei & Chen, 2010). Conversely, negative interactions with peers (e.g., peer rejection, peer victimisation, peer bullying), increases dissatisfaction among students towards their school. The importance of preventing negative peer experiences along with facilitating positive peer interaction cannot be overstated when building a positive school climate.

Adult–adult relationships among all staff at the school are also important, as are the collaborative relationships that the school cultivates with the community (Cohen et al., 2009). Kaplan Toren and Seginer (2015) discovered that the school climate is a predictor of healthy school–home relationships and in turn how involved parents are in their children's education. They found parental involvement to be a positive influence on junior high school students' self-evaluation and academic achievement. Cohen et al. (2009) suggest that this domain also includes a respect for diversity. This would directly impact students with disabilities and their experience at school.

Academic outcomes and supports

Academic outcomes and supports comprise different types of self-perceived supports a student receives from teachers to perform academically well and to achieve desired academic goals (Zullig et al., 2011). Students who receive different types of academic support feel a sense of academic futility, accomplishment and recognition, whereas those who struggle with academic assessments, assignments and homework perceive school as an unpleasant place (Danielsen, Samdal, Hetland & Wol, 2009; Suldo, Frank, Chappel, Albers & Bateman, 2014).

Teachers have been found to be the greatest source of different types of academic support for students at school (Zullig et al., 2010). When teachers hold high expectations of and belief in students' ability in addition to supporting them academically, students' self-efficacy is enhanced, as are their levels of school and life satisfaction (Danielsen et al., 2009). Academic support also facilitates higher academic achievement that further leads to academic competence (Danielsen et al., 2009).

Research suggests that autonomy-supportive teaching-learning practice can meet the support needs of students in school (Perlman, 2013). Autonomy-supportive practice entails allowing students the freedom to participate in the classroom decision making process (autonomy), valuing everyone as an equal and competent member of the classroom community (belongingness), providing reflective feedback rather than punitive measures, and setting high expectations (competence). This practice has been shown to make the classroom experience more satisfactory for students (Baker et al., 2003; Danielsen et al., 2009).

Physical environment

The physical environment domain refers to the school's facilities, such as: (a) size, (b) temperature, (c) lighting, (d) environmental safety, (e) cleanliness, (f) inviting aesthetic quality and décor, (g) ambient noise, (h) adequate space and materials and (i) curricular and extracurricular offerings (Cohen et al., 2009; Zullig et al., 2011).

There are various benefits to smaller schools for student achievement, safety, and relationships among members of the school community. Smaller schools are positively correlated to school connectedness (Grauer, 2012) and it has been suggested that smaller schools lead to improved academic performance (Stevenson, 2006). Because it is often unreasonable, if not impossible to reduce the size of a school, the school climate may benefit from the creation of small learning communities (Quint, 2006). School space can have an impact on students' feelings about safety, thereby affecting that domain also. Astor, Meyer and Pinter (2001) revealed that students felt unsafe in unsupervised areas of the school building. The Center for Social and Emotional Education (2010) explains that physical environment attributes such as classroom layout, activity schedules and student–teacher interactions can influence student behaviours and feelings of safety.

One tenet of this domain is that each person contributes to the care of the school, operationally and physically. Widely used as a part of the School Wide Positive Behavioural Interventions and Supports (SWPBIS) expectation of respecting property, students can be involved in caring for the school physically by keeping the classroom and school clean by throwing away unwanted items, cleaning up any spills, eating and drinking in designated areas, reporting any graffiti when they see it and returning any classroom or playground equipment to the proper areas (pbis.org, n.d.). They can be involved operationally through shared decision-making (Cohen et al., 2009).

Lastly, a positive school climate includes a physical layout that has been made accessible for all students. The environment should be adapted for those with mobility challenges, so that they can access all areas of the school (Coulston & Smith, 2013). Although an inclusive school is not just about the physical premises, it is still important that any inaccessible areas be identified and modified.

Classroom climate

By the 1990s researchers were focusing on classes and teachers (Griffith, 1995). Griffith suggested that if students were in a school where they changed classes, as in the typical high school model, then climate needed to be defined and examined school wide. If they stayed in one class all day, as is common in primary schools, then climate should be examined in regards to that class and teacher. Recent research by Kaplan et al. (2015) focused on classroom climate and parental involvement in students' education both at home and at school, and their effect on the self-evaluation and academic achievement of junior high school students in Israel.

Kaplan et al. (2015) state that classroom climate "relates to interpersonal relationships pertaining to teacher–student and to classroom peer relationships, and to the educational atmosphere set in part by the teacher and the students (e.g., learning opportunities, competition and cooperation) and in part by pedagogical considerations (such as task differentiation and grouping practices)" (p. 812). They also discuss three dimensions of classroom climate: teacher–student relationships, peer relationships and educational atmosphere. While these are well-aligned with the domains of school climate, since they are focused on the classroom, they present differently, as part of a student's total classroom experience.

Classroom experience is largely shaped by the teaching and learning practices used during class and the social environment of the classroom. Classroom practices should meet students' psychological needs for autonomy, competence and belongingness (Ryan & Deci, 2000). This should increase student satisfaction with the learning environment, thereby allowing them to enjoy school more (Tian, Chen & Huebner, 2014; Baker et al., 2003).

The teacher–student element consists of teacher awareness and response to the academic and emotional needs of students, and how much they value the students' interests, motivation and point of view. Kaplan et al. (2015) found that the quality of this relationship is a predictor of student behavioural and academic success. They also argued that teacher support affects students' behaviour, academic achievement and self-concept. The quality of peer relationships was important because students who felt supported by their peers had positive attitudes towards academic and social goals and better psychological adjustment. Conversely, low peer support is related to low self-esteem, higher depression and increased challenging behaviour. The educational atmosphere domain consists of learning opportunities, differentiation, competition, assessment techniques, grouping practices, behaviour management, and classroom organisation and instructional support. Overall Kaplan et al. (2015) found that classroom environment affects the level of parental involvement; parents were more likely to be involved in their children's education if the children perceived that their classroom had a positive environment.

School climate and students with disabilities

Studies focusing on school climate and students with disabilities are virtually non-existent. However, positive school climate includes providing quality support for teaching, learning, behaviour and anti-bullying in an inclusive environment. Coulston & Smith (2013) include inclusion as a focus of their definition for school climate: "School climate is the holistic context of the life, vigor, and quality of the social connectedness, physical elements, and supportive practices that nurture inclusion and safeness" (p. 1). Their philosophy is that each person wants to be socially and emotionally connected to school, and they suggest that school should be viewed as a home, rather than a place.

Students with disabilities are among the most marginalised group in educational settings and are more likely to experience bullying at school (U.S. Department of Education, 2015). Although national and global policies aim to protect this group from marginalisation and discrimination, they seem to have had little effect on bullying of students with disabilities in educational environments (U.S. Department of Education, 2015). Research examining the attitudes of students without disabilities has shown that overall they prefer to interact with children that do not possess physical or intellectual disabilities (Curcic, 2009). Students with disabilities commonly experience greater rejection from peers than students without disabilities (NSCC, 2007). This rejection can negatively affect the self-perceptions of students with disabilities, and in turn, these negative perceptions affect behaviour, relationships with peers and adults, school achievement and heath (NSCC, 2007). When an entire group of students in a school is marginalised in such a way, there is a need for significant improvement in school climate.

In order to improve their climates, schools need to focus on inclusivity. Ross (2013) posits that students and families must have full access to appropriately supported high expectations for achievement, emotionally and physically safe learning environments and caring relationships at school. He further states that this can be accomplished through increased understanding of diverse populations, reflective practice and having high expectations for all students. Bruns, Walrath, Glass-Siegel and Weist (2004) advocated for the addition of school-based mental health services, as their research found that the inclusion of such services improved school climate and reduced referrals to special education in the area of emotional and behavioural disorders.

Milsom (2006) discusses the importance of the attitudes towards students with disabilities of adults in educational environments. Research suggests that the attitudes of teachers, counsellors and school leaders directly influences whether or not students with disabilities are included in general education classes, curricula and activities (Curcic, 2009; Praisner, 2003). These findings highlight the need for professional development for all school staff, including leadership teams. This training should focus on disability awareness, behavioural interventions and how to facilitate successful social interactions between students with and without disabilities (Milsom, 2006). Facilitation can take the form of cooperative learning groups in the classroom, collaborative problem solving, peer tutoring and modelling from teachers on how to interact with a student with a disability. Milsom also recommends school-wide initiatives to promote and celebrate diversity.

School climate and connectedness

School connectedness, like school climate, has no agreed upon definition, and lacks an empirical base (Blum, 2005a). In fact, the term has been used synonymously with school climate (along with school attachment, school bonding and school engagement). This presents a cyclical dilemma when trying to define both constructs and when using school climate as a domain of school climate – students who feel connected have a more positive view of their school, but school must have a positive climate for students to feel connected.

The Centers for Disease Control (DASH-CDC, 2009) defined school connectedness as the extent to which a student feels that adults and peers with whom they have contact within their school care about them as individuals, their academic success and their overall well-being. It is clear from this definition that the largest factor related to school connectedness is the development of positive relationships among students, teachers and their peers. This is especially true for students with disabilities, who often struggle in school environments (McKenna, 2013; O'Brennan, Waasdorp & Bradshaw, 2014). Positive relationships with peers and adults at school are therefore crucial to both classroom climate and connectedness. This again illustrates the interdependency of not only school climate and school connectedness, but also of school climate's domains on each other.

Students who are unable to build positive relationships often suffer a lack of school connectedness, and frequently display challenging behaviour at school, which may result in overly harsh exclusionary discipline policies that further alienate and isolate them and breakdown their ability to form positive relationships with the adults at their school (Evans & Lester, 2012). So again, the problem is cyclical – a lack of connectedness causes problems that cause a further lack of connectedness.

Although the outcomes of a lack of connectedness are bleak, the outcomes of having a strong sense of connectedness are encouraging. School connectedness has been found to be a preventative intervention to combat several serious education-related issues: (a) the school-to-prison pipeline, (b) bullying, (c) school climate, (d) disciplinary practices and (e) engagement in health-risk behaviour (Evans & Lester, 2012; O'Brennan et al., 2014; Shippen, Patterson, Green & Smitherman, 2012; Waters, Cross & Shaw, 2010). Research suggests that interventions designed to promote positive relationships between students and teachers and peers show promise (Shippen et al., 2012). O'Brennan et al. (2014) suggest that to be effective, these interventions should be incorporated into programs that foster family involvement, are culturally responsive, involve community leaders from underrepresented groups and focus on bullying prevention. These are suggestions that are also often made as a result of research into school climate.

Gap between research, practice, and policy

The National School Climate Center (NSCC) was established in the USA in 1996 with a mission to support educational leaders in the field of social and emotional education. Over the years, their focus evolved, and their current mission is to assist schools in measuring and improving their climates for learning (NSCC, 2016a). NSCC (2007) identified a critical gap between the research on school climate and policy and practice in the field of education. They identify many research studies that demonstrate the significant effect that positive school climates have on student outcomes, but lament the fact that despite the availability of these options, policymakers have virtually ignored school climate measurement. NSCC suggests several reasons for this, the first being the aforementioned lack of a consistent definition of school climate. An absence of school climate leadership at the state level has also led to the failure of many policymakers to include school climate policy into educational accountability policy; it tends to remain isolated in health, special education and safety areas. Lastly, if the state or jurisdiction has no quality or improvement standards, it is unlikely that they are ready to link the use of data to improvement plans and technical assistance.

A gap between research and policy is detrimental, as it also results in gaps in educational practice and teacher education. As a result of a lack of policy on school climate improvement, most schools are not yet evaluating their climate using scientifically sound instruments, or they fail to measure all of the domains of school climate (NSCC, 2007). When data are not collected accurately, it is impossible to tell how closely a school is aligning its climate improvement efforts with research. A review of the literature reveals no systemic studies of these efforts.

The gap between research and teacher education programs may be attributed to more than simply a lack in policy. Many teacher education programs are constructed in such a way that preservice and early career teachers are so focused on learning pedagogy, they fail to recognise the importance of improving the quality of the climate in their classrooms and schools. Many programs have a heavy emphasis on literacy and numeracy, since these are the two areas globally that students are likely to be tested in. This may cause courses to neglect to provide teacher education students with important information on the significance of nurturing caring relationships with their students. NSCC (2007) deems that the incorporation of research-based information regarding school climate into teacher preparation courses as well as courses for educational leaders and school counsellors would be a significant advancement in the movement to eliminate the research to practice gap.

Although there is evidence of policies focused on school improvement globally (Seifert & Hartnell-Young, 2015; The United Nations, 1989; U.S. Department of Education, 2010), school climate is either not mentioned or mentioned in only a very broad sense. In order for policy to be effective, it should ensure that schools are accountable in the area of school climate as a component of school improvement. Policies should include a framework for improvement that incorporates scientifically sound assessments designed to measure all of the domains of school climate in order to facilitate data collection. The data collected should then be used to create school improvement plans and evaluate their implementation.

Improving school climate

Cohen et al. (2009) suggest that guidelines to improve school climate align with four key dimensions that promote a climate of learning: (a) a supportive learning community; (b) systematic approaches to supporting safety and positive behaviour; (c) involvement of families, students, school staff, and the surrounding community and (d) standards and measures to support continual improvement based on data. School leaders, teachers and other school staff can improve each of these dimensions through the implementation of school- and classroom-wide interventions.

Positive relationships among students, teachers, and other members of the school community are very significant influencers of school climate (Petrie, 2014); so building a supportive learning community should begin with strengthening relationships. School practices should support students to exercise self-determination, be given chances to have leadership roles and feel able to share their perceptions freely and readily. All stakeholders should be involved in the school improvement process and the implementation and assessment of interventions. A dually tiered behavioural and learning support system such as Positive Behaviour Interventions and Supports (PBIS)/Response to Intervention (RtI) will enable school personnel to support all learners regardless of challenges, respond quickly to any problems, and provide for those with chronic behaviour issues with intensive assessment and accommodations. The evidence based strategies included in this system support engagement and re-engagement (PBIS). PBIS also provides a framework from which to design a systematic approach to support safety and positive behaviours.

School leaders and teachers should seek to increase and/or improve home-school and community connections. Organising and assisting students and families in gaining access to special assistance and community services, as part of a wrap around model, will improve home–school–community relationships by making everyone feel welcome (NSCC, 2009). School leaders can facilitate the creation of supportive learning environments by providing a high quality operational infrastructure, sufficient staffing, and professional development.

School improvement should be guided by a set of standards and informed by the continual collection and analysis of data. The National School Climate Standards were developed by the National School Climate Center (2009) and complement the National Standards for Content, Leadership, and Professional Development and the Parent Teacher Associations National Standards for Family School Partnership. The Standards provide a blueprint in the form of a framework for school improvement, based on the tenets of a positive school climate. The framework consists of five standards to support school improvement:

1. A vision and plan, shared by the school community, for creating and sustaining a positive school climate.
2. School policies that promote social, emotional, ethical, civic and intellectual skills, knowledge, and engagement, a comprehensive system of learning support and ways to re-engage disengaged students.
3. School practices designed to promote learning and positive development of students, engagement in teaching, learning and school activities, address barriers to teaching and learning, re-engage those who have become disengaged and sustain an operational infrastructure that supports these practices.
4. The creation of a school environment where all community members feel safe and supported physically, emotionally and socially.
5. School-wide practices should be based on social justice and promote civic and social responsibilities.

Coulston and Smith (2013) believe that school leaders should survey students to assess the school climate, in order to create a baseline from which to begin school improvement efforts. They recommend the use of the *Comprehensive School Climate Inventory (CSCI)*, a scientifically sound survey that assesses the extent students, parents and school personnel feel safe, connected and engaged in school life. The CSCI is also connected to a web-based system that allows schools to administer the survey and use the data to inform school improvement efforts (NSCC, 2016b).

Conclusion

School climate and school connectedness are inextricably linked to one another, as school connectedness is considered a domain of school climate, and students in educational environments with positive school climate are more connected to their schools. Although there has been a call to determine an operational definition of school climate, this has not happened as of this writing, but most of the literature agrees that school climate consists of safety, relationships, academic outcomes and supports, the school's physical environment and school connectedness. School connectedness as a domain of school climate is focused on relationships, as the definition presented here centres on student perceptions of how others care about them. The frameworks and research presented in this chapter highlight relationship building as the strongest factor of school climate improvement, although this topic is often ignored or under-represented teaching certification programmes.

The National School Climate Center in the USA has been in existence for over a decade, making strides in promoting positive school climates that are "safe supportive environments that nurture social and emotional, ethical, and academic skills" (http://www.schoolclimate.org/about/). They have provided research-based guidelines to support schools in assessing and improving their climates. There is a movement in other countries such as Australia and the United Kingdom to draw attention to the importance of school climate, and much of the literature and materials from those countries reference the work of the NSCC. This is a promising development, and may mean that we are coming closer globally to an agreement on the definition and importance of school climate and hopefully policies that will translate to best practice.

THEORY TO PRACTICE

Suggestions can be divided into four areas:
Policymakers can...

- Recognise the connection between climate, school improvement and academic achievement
- Create national, state and local policies that include climate and school improvement in educational accountability systems
- Enact policy that provides consistency and accuracy in the definition and measurement of school climate
- Provide for defined climate leadership at the state level in education

Teacher educators can...

- Introduce school climate and supporting research at an appropriate point in the curriculum for preservice and inservice teachers, administrators and other relevant staff

- Provide the preservice teachers with the opportunity to practise assessing and improving school climate during their fieldwork experience
- Deliver a comprehensive curriculum that includes social, emotional and ethical learning in addition to academics

School leaders can...

- Be aware of evidence-based practices to measure and improve school climate
- Encourage and support the use of scientifically sound school climate assessment tools to provide a baseline for improving school climate
- Promote a network of schools and communities committed to improving school climate
- Contribute to research that supports efforts in the field to improve best practices in school climate
- Provide a variety of integrated academic and behavioural interventions for students with and at risk for chronic behaviour problems

Teachers can...

- Increase collaboration with families, especially those who have children who engage in frequent misbehaviour
- Provide positive reinforcement to all students, especially those who engage in frequent misbehaviour
- Call home when students are doing well in order to highlight positive behaviours
- Be aware of and respond to students' academic and emotional needs, and value students' interests, motivation and point of view
- Support active engagement for students with diverse abilities
- Encourage positive social interactions among all students

4

ASSESSING STUDENT SCHOOL CONNECTEDNESS

As previously established, school connectedness can be defined as the extent to which a student feels that adults and peers, present in their academic environment, care about them as individuals, their academic success and their overall well-being (DASH-CDC, 2009). Four sub-components, school bonding, school attachment, school engagement and school climate, have been identified. Students with disabilities typically have low levels of school connectedness, as they often experience difficulty in establishing and maintaining positive relationships with peers and adults in authority, have poor academic outcomes and are less engaged in the classroom than their typically developing peers (Lane, Carter, Pierson & Glaeser, 2006). Those who experience negative school climates are often also subject to exclusionary discipline polices, which negatively affects their level of connectedness to their school (DASH-CDC, 2009; Eriksson, Welander & Granlund, 2007).

In order to design comprehensive interventions to build levels of connectedness in all areas for students with disabilities, it is important to assess their individual levels of school connectedness. Effective assessment may also provide valuable information to help determine the type of educational setting (general education classroom, pull-out programme or self-contained classroom) that would best foster school connectedness in individual students. Libbey (2004) suggests that measuring school connectedness may be difficult, as there is currently a dearth of assessments for school connectedness that incorporate each of the four sub-components identified here (e.g., school bonding, school attachment, school engagement, school climate). This is due to a lack of agreement on both the term used to describe connectedness and a definition of school connectedness. Terms that are frequently used that have the same or a related meaning include: school attachment, school bonding, school climate, school connection, school engagement, school involvement, student satisfaction with school and teacher support. These terms are present in both health and education literature, and each have been shown to be highly correlated with student outcomes.

Separate constructs of school connectedness have been measured throughout the literature using specific assessments that separately measure school bonding, school climate, school attachment or school engagement (Zullig, Huebner & Patton, 2011). However, they do not combine the subcomponents of school connectedness (L'Engle & Jackson, 2008). A comprehensive assessment that measures all aspects of school connectedness would enable researchers and educators to access accurate information for use in the design of school connectedness strategies and evidenced-based practices for students with disabilities (DASH-CDC, 2009; Chapman et al., 2013; Libbey, 2004; Thapa et al., 2013). The following is a discussion on the importance of assessing school connectedness, followed by a discussion of studies that assessed the different aspects of school connectedness, the measurements they employed, and the results and implications for future research and practice.

Importance of school connectedness and assessment

McNeely, Nonnemaker and Blum (2002) analysed data from the National Longitudinal Study of Adolescent Health (Add Health), a survey of a nationally representative sample of U.S. adolescents in grades 7 through 12 during the 1994–1995 school year. Add Health is the only nationally (U.S.) representative dataset on school connectedness and school attributes. They looked at the results of the five items on the student survey that dealt with school connectedness specifically, along with structural and environmental features of schools linked to the developmental needs of adolescents, and found that school connectedness was positively associated with diminished involvement in adolescent health-risk behaviours. They identified classroom management climate, school size, severity of discipline policies and participation in extra-curricular activities as factors of school connectedness that are open to change. They also discovered that some schools have actually changed these factors and thus improved levels of student connectedness. They concluded that school connectedness is the only school-related variable that is protective for every single health risk outcome. Seven years later, the Centers for Disease Control and Prevention (DASH-CDC, 2009) underscored the importance of school connectedness, as there is a positive correlation between school connectedness and academic success and healthy behaviours. They identified adult support, positive peer relations, commitment to education and environment as four components of school connectedness to be assessed. See Figure 2.1 for a visual representation of how these four components relate to the four listed above.

Best practice dictates that the factors of school connectedness in a school be assessed in order to design interventions that improve the connectedness of students with disabilities to their schools, and therefore, improving the outcomes of this vulnerable population.

Assessing the components of school connectedness

School bonding

School bonding refers to the connections that young people have with their schools and their learning, and is comprised of attachment (emotionally linked to school) and commitment (investment in the group) (Libbey, 2004; Maddox & Prinz, 2003). School bonding has also has been known to include involvement and belief in school rules. Some scholars have divided attachment into two separate experiences – those with school and those with people, and these are reflected in the development of assessments to measure school bonding. Maddox and Prinz (2003) suggest that it is important to assess this construct, as there is a strong linkage between school bonding and student outcomes, and school bonding is responsive to intervention through the modification of the school environment. Typical measures of school bonding include student self-reports, teacher reports and structured interviews, but self-report is used most often. Unfortunately, many of the studies described in the literature employ measures of school bonding that have not been proven to be reliable or valid (Whiteside-Mansell et al., 2015).

Maddox & Prinz (2003) postulate that school bonding assessment instruments must measure the four dimensions of school bonding suggested by Murray and Greenberg (2001): attachment to school, attachment to personnel, school commitment and school involvement. They reviewed three measurements of school bonding (*Effective School Battery, What About You Scales*; *The Psychological Sense of School Membership Scale*; and *Adapted People in My Life Scale*), but found that none were exclusively focused on school bonding. In order to use any of them to measure school bonding, individual items or parts of the instruments had to be extracted. Other issues were lack of strong reliability (*Effective School Battery*), and the fact that none of the measurements analysed covered all of the key dimensions of school bonding. They called for the creation and validation of a measure devoted completely to school bonding to improve the comprehensiveness of school bonding assessment, as well as research in the area. They cautioned that the measures should be age-related, as facets of school bonding differ depending on the developmental stage of the students being evaluated.

More recent literature would suggest that this call has been answered, at least partially. Whiteside-Mansell et al. (2015) examined the psychometric properties of three school bonding assessment tools, then combined them to create a shorter instrument. They found that although the instruments were psychometrically sound, their length was arduous. The concepts within school bonding that they measured were attachment (ties that students have to their schools, including peer and teacher relationships), commitment (the investment students have in school and the importance of school in their lives), belief in school rules (students' attitudes and opinions about discipline, especially in regard to fairness), and involvement (students' participation in school and classroom activities). Thus they chose three instruments that measured these four constructs, were used with adolescents and had strong face validity. These were: Jenkin's (1997) *School Bonding*, the *School Connection Scale* (Brown & Evans, 2002) and *School Connectedness*, by Resnick et al. (1997). After examining each scale and determining each was psychometrically sound, they combined the items of each, removed redundancies, and developed the *Brief Survey of School Bonding*. Whiteside-Mansell et al. (2015) claim that this tool is concise, comprehensive and psychometrically sound, and can be used to evaluate the impact of school-based interventions on school bonding of adolescents.

Although progress is being made, there remains a need for valid and reliable instruments that measure school bonding. Although the recent development of the *Brief Survey of School Bonding* is promising, there remains a need for an instrument that measures the school bonding of younger students. Context is another factor that should be taken into account, as existing measurements may not be valid for measuring the school bonding of students with disabilities in special programs or schools, incarcerated youth and/or young people in other special settings such as hospitals or mental health centres.

School attachment

School attachment is commonly used as a term for the connection students feel with their school. Research suggests that this connection is positively associated with students' academic motivation, classroom behaviour and social competence (Dornbusch, Erickson, Laird & Wong, 2001). It has been used as a separate factor as well as part of a larger concept (Libbey, 2004). Measuring school attachment has traditionally occurred as part of a subscale of a larger assessment, as it is normally viewed as one part of a larger construct (Goodenow, 1993; Jenkins, 1997; Moody & Bearman, 2001), usually measured with three to four items, rather than with a purpose-built instrument. Research has indicated its importance to students' behaviour, motivation and academic achievement (Johnson, Crosnoe & Thaden, 2006), garnering interest in its identification and measurement in order to design interventions to improve the school attachment of at-risk students.

Dornbusch et al. (2001) used Add Health data to examine the effect of family and school attachment on adolescent health risk and deviant behaviour. They used the school connectedness composite developed by Resnick et al. (1997), which comprised eight items. This again highlights the lack of agreement of terms and definitions, as they used a school connectedness scale to measure school attachment. They found that school connectedness (attachment) was strongly linked to the start of a pattern of deviant behaviour, but not the intensity of the behaviour.

Johnson et al. (2006) also used data from the Add Health study to determine that not only is school attachment reduced as a student progresses from primary to secondary school, but also that this is more prominent in girls than boys. Girls experienced greater risks to their mental health at this age, as they become more self-conscious and more dissatisfied with themselves and their bodies. This gender reversal was only significant for white students, not black, Hispanic, or Asian students. Interestingly, girls continue to achieve well academically, earning higher grades than boys in both upper and lower grade levels. This was explained by the fact that school attachment is related more strongly to grades for boys than girls, particularly in the upper grade levels. The authors clarified that this could also be due to higher drop out rates for boys; the boys least attached to school had probably already left, raising the school attachment levels for the gender. They suggested that consideration of the intersection of gender and race in adolescents' level of school attachment is necessary, rather than the current sole focus on academic achievement.

Research has shown that students who like school achieve better academically, have less disciplinary problems, higher attendance rates and lower rates of dropping out than their peers who dislike school (Hallinan, 2008). One way to improve these outcomes is to assess school attachment levels, along with other factors and implement interventions designed to increase these levels. It should be noted, however, that since school attachment is rarely regarded as a separate construct, but part of a larger one, measurement of attachment usually consists of a number of items from a larger instrument measuring a broader concept, such as school climate or school connectedness.

School engagement

School engagement is a term used to describe students' relationship with school, specifically in the area of academic motivation. This refers to how many hours students spend doing homework, along with their grades and test scores (Libbey, 2004). Some research studies expand upon this definition and also include attendance, preparation for class, teacher perceptions, self-regulated and disruptive behaviour, how much a student likes school, if the student sees school as useful to their future, and a student's sense of alienation while at school. To measure school engagement, students are generally asked to answer questions such as, "I want to do well at this school", "I pay attention in class", and "I take school seriously" on a Likert scale (Libbey, 2004). Students become more disengaged with school as they progress to higher grades; up to 40% of youth are currently disengaged with school (Yazzie-Mintz, 2007). This is especially true of young people from disadvantaged backgrounds. Studying student engagement may help to improve this statistic, provide us with answers to low achievement, student boredom, alienation and drop out rates.

Conducting research in the area of school engagement can be challenging, as Fredricks and McColskey (2012) pointed out that a large variation in the different definitions and measurements of school engagement makes it difficult to compare findings across studies. There is variation in terms (school engagement, student engagement, academic engagement) and subcomponents (some scholars include behaviour and emotion, some behaviour, emotion and a cognitive component). Although Reschly and Christenson (2006) conceptualised four dimensions: academic, behavioural, cognitive and psychological (affective) engagement, most scholars agree that the first three are the definitive dimensions of school engagement. The behavioural dimension comprises participation in academic, social and/or extracurricular activities, following rules, skipping school, inappropriate behaviour. The emotional dimension involves reactions to teachers, classmates, academics, school and belonging. The last dimension, cognitive, includes a student's level of investment in learning and exerting the necessary effort to master skills (Fredricks & McColskey, 2012).

The various dimensions lend themselves to different methods of assessing student engagement. The most common, student self-reports, have items that are mostly general, but some assess engagement in specific subjects, such as reading or math. They are considered to be superior to observation or teacher rating scales because they measure things that are not observable, or that must be inferred from observation (Fredricks & McColskey, 2012). Other advantages include the ability to assess large samples of students at low cost, making it possible to compare across schools (Appleton, Christenson & Furlong, 2008). The main disadvantage of this method is that students may not answer honestly. Ensuring their identities remain anonymous and assuring them of this may increase the rate of honest answers.

Experience Sampling (ESM) is another method of assessing engagement. It entails students carrying pagers or alarm watches, and filling out a self-report questionnaire about their location, activities and cognitive and affective responses at the moment they receive a signal from the device (Hektner, Schmidt & Csikszentmihalyi, 2007). This method allows for collection of engagement in the moment rather than retrospectively like student self-reports. The disadvantage of this method is that it requires a large time investment for the student participants, and they must be able and willing to comply when they receive the signal.

A third method, teacher ratings of students, involves teachers rating each student's engagement and participation, and averaging scores across students in the class (Fredricks & McColskey, 2012). Teacher rating scales typically assess both behavioural and emotional engagement, although some also assess cognitive domains. This method is good for measuring the school engagement of younger students who are unable to complete self-reports, or students with low literacy. Several studies include both student and teacher reports (Skinner, Marchand, Furrer & Kindermann, 2008) in order to see correlations between the two. These comparisons generally show more correspondence between behavioural engagement rather than emotional, as behaviour is observable, while emotions need to be inferred from behaviour.

Some researchers use structured or semi-structured interviews as their method of assessing school engagement. Interview data provide insight into the reasons for variability in levels of engagement to understand why some students are engaged while others are disengaged (Blumenfeld et al., 2005). Data from interviews can provide a detailed account of how students construct meaning about their school experiences. Although interviews can provide rich data, they also have a few disadvantages. Interviewer bias and knowledge can impact the quality of the data, and there may be problems with the reliability and validity of the findings (Blumenfeld et al., 2005).

Observations are used to assess on and off task student behaviours to assess academic engagement (Fredricks & McColskey, 2012). An observer uses momentary time sampling to record rates of student behaviour, such as: asking and answering questions, reading aloud, writing, completing assignments and talking about academics. This method is sometimes used to screen children for special needs support, as it provides detailed and descriptive accounts of contextual factors occurring with engagement levels. This method may be best employed to verify information collected from surveys and interviews, as there are several disadvantages such as: (a) it can be time consuming, as observation must occur across different subjects and activities, (b) there are reliability and generalisability issues, (c) the data provides limited information on effort, participation, or thinking and (d) the quality of the data collected depends upon the skill of the observer (Fredricks & McColskey, 2012).

Fredricks & McColskey (2012) examined instruments that assess student engagement. They reported on 11 instruments; only five of those covered all three dimensions of school engagement. Some instruments were a subset of a larger instrument, and they were used for a variety of purposes: (a) to evaluate school reform efforts, (b) to study the relationship between context and engagement, (c) to determine the ways that parents, peers and communities influence students' school engagement, (d) to evaluate drop out prevention interventions, (e) to monitor engagement in a school and identify areas that need improvement, (f) to assess the extent to which students identify or disengage with school, (g) to compare school scores to a national sample and (h) to identify struggling students who are at risk for disengagement and academic failure. These different purposes underscore the importance of careful definition of the dimensions of school engagement and how they operationalise them. Glanville and Wildhagen (2007) expanded on this, positing that developmental and other characteristics influence school engagement, so they should be accounted for in assessment by conducting confirmatory factor analysis to validate surveys for different ages, races, gender and socio-economic status. Assessing school engagement enables one to focus on contextual factors that can be targeted for intervention rather than focusing on individual characteristics. This would require questions on instruments to be less general and more domain-specific. Overall, it is recommended that multiple methods are the best way to measure school engagement (Appleton et al., 2008).

School climate

School climate is a multidimensional construct that is linked to student achievement, aggression, bullying, crime, attachment, bonding, connectedness, engagement and alcohol and drug use (Zullig et al., 2011). Similar to the constructs listed above, and school connectedness in general, there is a lack of consensus in the literature, policy and practice documents on the definition of school climate (Gage et al., 2016). However, most definitions include the dimensions of relationships, safety, instructional practices, academic outcomes and the organisational structure of schools (Cohen, McCabe, Michelli & Pickeral, 2009). The U.S. National School Climate Center (n.d.) suggests that school climate is the sum of students', staff's and parents' perceptions of the school experience. Some of the definitions of school climate include the domain of connectedness, demonstrating how school climate and school connectedness are inextricably linked to one another.

Assessing school climate is the first step in the implementation of school improvement efforts, as it provides a baseline from which to begin (Coulston & Smith, 2013). A review of the literature reveals a multitude of validated and self-created school climate measurements (Kohl, Recchia & Steffgen, 2013). Although most of the available assessments are self-report surveys, other methods such as school audits, walk-throughs, checklists, observation, grades, attendance rates and behavioural reports can also be used to measure school climate (Kohl et al., 2013). The National School Climate Center (n.d.) suggests that the best approach to measure school climate is to use different methods and triangulate them for a more comprehensive picture. Several of the most frequently used instruments are described below.

Psycho-Social Environment Profile (PSE) (WHO, 2013) was designed to assess seven areas of school climate (providing a friendly, rewarding and supportive atmosphere; supporting cooperation and active learning; forbidding physical punishment and violence; not tolerating bullying, harassment and discrimination; valuing the development of creative activity; connecting school and the home life; and promoting equal opportunities and participation). This assessment tool is intended to be used by a diverse range of school personnel, including administrators, custodial staff, secretarial staff, volunteers, cafeteria staff, teachers, community leaders and members of school health teams. The PSE Profile aims to identify and change conditions that can increase the school's capacity to be supportive and to promote learning and development. The instrument, along with scoring instructions and discussion sheets, is available online at no cost.

The Organisation for Economic Co-operation and Development's (OECD) Teaching and Learning International Survey (TALIS) is the first study designed to examine the working conditions of teachers and the learning environment in schools on an international scale (OECD, 2016). It was created through an international collaboration of public authorities and aims to help countries review and develop policies for the teacher labour market, school effectiveness, teacher professional development and feedback and evaluation systems for the teaching workforce. It was first conducted in 2008, in 200 schools in each of 24 countries over five continents, and surveyed secondary principals and teachers about school leadership, teacher evaluation and feedback, professional development, and teacher beliefs, attitudes and practices. It was repeated in 2013 in 34 countries in primary and secondary schools, and there are plans for a third survey in 2018. The instrument can be taken online or on paper and takes 45 minutes to complete. The data from the surveys were used to create publications that offer strategies for improvement in the areas of instructional quality, teacher professional development, classroom teaching practices and school leadership (OECD, 2016).

The U.S. National School Climate Center recommend the use of the *Comprehensive School Climate Inventory (CSCI)*, a valid and reliable survey that assesses 12 dimensions across four areas: safety, teaching and learning, interpersonal relationships and institutional environment. It incorporates the perceptions of students (3rd–12th grade), school personnel and parents. The CSCI is available in several languages, takes 15–20 minutes, and can be paper- or web-based (NSCC, 2016b). The cost of administering the instrument is dependent upon the size of the school.

The School Climate Assessment Instrument (SCAI) was created by the Alliance for the Study of School Climate (ASSSC) (ASSC, 2016). It is commercially available for both primary and secondary schools and has eight subscales: (a) physical appearance, (b) faculty relations, (c) student interactions, (d) leadership and decision making, (e) discipline and management, (f) learning, instruction and assessment, (g) attitude and culture and (h) community relations. Special education is available as an optional dimension, as is project-based learning. There are teacher, student and parent versions of the survey, and the results of each can be cross-referenced and compared. Rather than using a Likert-scale like the majority of other surveys, the SCAI employs an analytic trait structure that presents the participant with three options that represent three levels of phenomena. This enables a description of the range of conditions that exist in a school. A study conducted by Gangi (2010) found the SCAI to be a valid and reliable school climate assessment instrument when compared to other leading assessments.

The ED School Climate Surveys (EDSCLS) (National Center on Safe Supportive Learning Environments, 2016) are a suite of survey instruments developed for schools, school districts and states by the U.S. Department of Education's National Center for Education Statistics (NCES). The survey platform is free of charge, and produces school-, district-, and state-level scores on 13 topics within three domains of school climate: engagement (cultural and linguistic competence, relationships, school participation), safety (emotional safety, physical safety, bullying, substance abuse, emergency readiness), and environment (physical and instructional environments, physical and mental health, discipline). The surveys are appropriate for all levels of schooling, and include the perspectives of students, teachers and staff and parents. The EDSCLS were pilot tested and found to be psychometrically sound. One possible disadvantage of this instrument is the number of items. The student surveys consist of 74 items; school staff surveys have 137, while the parent surveys have 47 items.

While this is by no means an exhaustive list of available school climate scales, it shows that there are a number of instruments that can be used by both researchers and schools to investigate school climate. They have several characteristics in common: self-reporting; including the dimensions of relationships, safety, instructional practices and school environment; and all but the TALIS include the perspectives of students, school staff and parents. It is important for researchers and practitioners to choose instruments that meet their needs, for example, an instrument that fits a specific theoretical model of school climate for a research study, or an instrument that fits the financial, contextual and age characteristics of a school.

School connectedness assessments

The ambiguity of what exactly constitutes school connectedness and its sub-components presents a challenge when it comes to assessment. Instruments assessing school connectedness should assess the four subcomponents (school bonding, school attachment, school engagement and school climate), be reliable and valid, be user-friendly, and include the perspectives of all stakeholders. A review of the literature revealed eight instruments that met these requirements (see Table 4.1 for details). Researchers, based on literature in the field, constructed all eight. Two of the instruments' titles suggested that they measured school climate, but had scales within that measured school connectedness. Only one, the *School Connectedness Scale* (Hendrickson Lohmeier & Lee, 2011), actually used the term in its title. Other assessments used the terms school membership, school engagement, school connection and school relationship in their titles.

Each of the eight identified instruments was examined to determine if they measure the four components of school connectedness suggested by the DASH-CDC (2009): adult support, positive peer relations, commitment to education and environment. The results of this examination are provided in Table 4.2. Only three instruments: the *School Climate Measure* (Zullig et al., 2010), the *School Connectedness Scale* (Hendrickson Lohmeier & Lee, 2011) and the *School Connection Scale* (Brown & Leigh, 2000) measured all of the components. All three of these instruments were designed for and used with students in secondary school (Grade 6 and higher). As research indicates that students' sense of connectedness to their schools wanes as they progress to higher grades (Johnson et al., 2006), an instrument that measures the school connectedness of students in primary school would provide more insight into this phenomenon. Researchers and practitioners should consider their context as well as their specific needs (what they are evaluating or endeavouring to predict) when choosing an appropriate instrument to measure school connectedness.

Conclusion

Increased interest in student well-being and connectedness with school over the past two decades has led to the establishment of a rich research base and improved policy and practice in the area internationally. Unfortunately, there is still a lack of consensus in the terminology and definition of school connectedness and its sub-components. This presents a challenge when assessing the school connectedness of students. School connectedness could be assessed by measuring each of its components separately, but this method has the potential to be chaotic and time consuming for the assessors and the participants. A more effective and expedient method is employing a comprehensive school connectedness assessment, such as one of the three mentioned above.

Old school paradigms don't address the complex needs of today's students, and more focus needs to be put on relationships and connections. The majority of research

TABLE 4.1 Assessments of school connectedness

Name of assessment	What was measured	Who was surveyed	Evidence	Results
Comprehensive School Climate Inventory	Staff, Parent, and Student surveys; 13 items each, measuring: safety, teaching and learning, interpersonal relationships, social media, and the institutional environment	U.S. national sample: 2,454 high school, 5,182 middle school, and 520 upper elementary school students, 315 parents of elementary students, 683 parents of middle schoolers, and 258 parents of high school students, 358 elementary teaching/professional staff, 692 middle school staff, and 529 high school staff	Guo et al. (2011) National School Climate Center, n.d.	All forms of the CSCI show good construct validity and strong internal consistency.
Psychological Sense of School Membership (PSSM) scale	18 items measuring School membership: Caring relationships, acceptance, rejection	755 middle and junior high school students in the Northeast United States 504 Australian high school students	Goodenow (1993) You et al. (2011)	School membership was substantially correlated to school motivation, and to a lesser degree with grades and with teacher-rated effort. The PSSM is a multidimensional instrument, measuring the three factors that influence students' perceptions of their school membership: caring relationships, acceptance and rejection.

(continued)

TABLE 4.1 continued

Name of assessment	What was measured	Who was surveyed	Evidence	Results
School Climate Measure	39 items measuring school climate: Positive Student–Teacher Relationships, School Connectedness, Academic Support, Order and Discipline, School Physical Environment, School Social Environment, Perceived Exclusion/Privilege, and Academic Satisfaction	2,049 students from three school districts in a U.S. Midwestern state	Zullig, Koopman, Patton & Ubbes (2010)	Identified 8 school climate domains; positive correlation between positive student–teacher relationships and the other school climate domains and a negative correlation between perceived exclusion/privilege and school connectedness.
School Connectedness Scale (SCS)	54 items: relationship with school, adults and peers crossed with 3 levels of connectedness	260 students in grades 9–12 in the USA	Hendrickson Lohmeier & Lee (2011)	High reliability and validity, powerful evaluation tool.
Student School Engagement Measure (SSEM)	22 items: aspirations, productivity, belonging	370 8th grade students at 3 middle schools in the central mountain region of the USA	Hazel et al. (2014)	Found that the SSEM is a measure of engagement, but not life satisfaction.
School Relationship Questionnaire	11 items: Relationship with school, Relationship with teachers and Relationship with peers	Sample 1: 15,546 U.S. adolescents from grades 6 to 10, from a representative U.S. student population Sample 2: 574 Chinese students in grades 7 and 10, from two large urban areas in Northeast China	Dong et al. (2012)	Exploratory factor analyses resulted in three subscales, and this result was consistent across countries.
The School Connection Scale	16 items: school connectedness: perceived power in school, belief in the validity of the institution, importance of school to individual goals, social/emotional attachment to those at school	1,739 secondary students (Grades 7–12) from California, USA	Brown & Leigh (2000)	Predictive validity was consistent when comparing the association with substance abuse, school participation, and school grades.

TABLE 4.2 Connectedness assessments and measured domains

Assessment	Total number of items	Adult support	Positive peer relationships	Commitment to education	Environment
Comprehensive School Climate Inventory (CSCI)	Staff, Parent, and Student surveys; 13 items each	x	x		x
Psychological Sense of School Membership (PSSM) scale	18	x	x		x
School Climate Measure	39	x	x	x	x
School Connectedness Scale (SCS)	54	x	x	x	x
Student School Engagement Measure (SSEM)	22	x	x	x	
School Relationship Questionnaire	12	x	x		x
The School Connection Scale	16	x	x	x	x

focuses on how schools affect academic achievement, but not how it affects students' well-being and future success. As more evidence of the importance of school connectedness in relation to student outcomes emerges, it reinforces the fundamental need for effective assessment in order to plan intervention for improvement. Assessing school connectedness shifts the focus to contextual factors that can be targeted for intervention rather than focusing on individual characteristics.

THEORY TO PRACTICE

Suggestions can be divided into four areas:
    Policymakers can...

- Recognise the connection between school connectedness and student outcomes
- Create national, state, and local policies that include school connectedness assessment as a priority

- Enact policy that provides consistency and accuracy in the definition and measurement of school connectedness

Teacher educators can...

- Introduce school connection and supporting research at an appropriate point in the curriculum for preservice and inservice teachers, administrators, and other relevant staff
- Provide the preservice teachers with the opportunity to practise assessing and school connectedness during their fieldwork experience
- Deliver a comprehensive curriculum that includes social, emotional and ethical learning in addition to academics

School leaders can...

- Be aware of evidence-based practices to measure and improve school connectedness
- Encourage and support the use of scientifically sound school connectedness assessment tools to provide a baseline for improving school climate
- Involve all stakeholders in the assessment process – students, school staff and families
- Contribute to research that supports efforts in the field to improve best practices in assessing school connectedness
- Use the data from school connectedness measures to plan effective interventions to improve school climate

Teachers can...

- Encourage and support students in completing school connectedness self-reports
- Support active engagement in the assessment process for students with diverse abilities
- Become involved in the school connectedness assessment process
- Assist school leaders in using the data garnered from assessment to plan and implement strategies that will increase students' level of connectedness with their schools

5

CHARACTERISTICS OF STUDENTS WITH DISABILITIES THAT IMPACT SCHOOL CONNECTEDNESS

Students with disabilities typically experience difficulties with academics in the school setting, which may cause feelings of failure and isolation, negatively impacting their feeling of connectedness to their schools. In addition to academic challenges, many students with disabilities also struggle with the socioemotional and behavioural aspects of schooling (Furlong et al., 2004; Gresham & Kern, 2004; Kauffman & Landrum, 2013; Kern, 2015; Lane et al., 2006). They may have problems creating and maintaining relationships with their teachers and peers due to impulsiveness and misread social cues. This can, in turn, lead to misbehaviour. Students who demonstrate high levels of inappropriate behaviour in school are often the recipients of exclusionary discipline practices (Evans & Lester, 2012; Gresham, 2002; Lane et al., 2006; Rivkin, 2009). Exclusion from school contributes to the development of poor relationships with teachers and peers, and puts these students at an increased risk for developing depression and anxiety and may lead to decreased satisfaction with school, school dropout and health risk behaviours. These in turn may lead to poor outcomes such as involvement in violent crimes, substance abuse and incarceration in adulthood.

This chapter will examine the characteristics of disabilities that may impact students' perception of school connectedness. The components of school connectedness that specifically impact on the lives of students with disabilities are discussed, including relationships, classroom engagement, discipline policies and behaviour management. Risk and protective factors for this vulnerable population will be examined in order to make recommendations for practice.

Students with disabilities and school connectedness

School connectedness is typically organised into four components: (a) the development of teacher–student relationships, (b) positive peer relationships,

(c) educational commitment and (d) safe and positive school environments (DASH-CDC, 2009). Students with disabilities often have difficulties in all of these areas, especially when it comes to establishing and maintaining relationships with peers and teachers (Murray & Greenberg, 2006). The quality of relationships between this population and caregivers such as parents and teachers will negatively or positively affect their functioning and social emotional adjustment. Although this is most prevalent in early childhood, it carries on to early adolescence also (Murray & Greenburg, 2006). Shochet, Dadds, Ham and Montague (2006) discovered that school connectedness is associated with both positive and negative outcomes for students with disabilities. Positive outcomes included: peer support, teacher support, academic motivation and higher achievement. Negative outcomes comprised: depressive symptoms, low self-esteem, low optimism, paranoia, distrust of others, social withdrawal and loneliness.

Adolescence is a time of change and vulnerability for all young people, but is often even more difficult for students with disabilities, who experience heightened vulnerability compared to their typically developing peers (Al-Yago, 2016). This vulnerability stems from the fact that they are more likely to experience peer rejection, depression, anxiety, behavioural problems, involvement with juvenile justice, poor academics, drop out and poor adult outcomes than their typically developing peers (Murray & Greenberg, 2006). These negative experiences are frequently associated with the characteristics of their disability. Although many of these characteristics overlap, the research in the field is commonly categorical, so will be discussed in that manner below.

Learning disabilities and Attention Deficit Hyperactivity Disorder

Learning disabilities (LD) are the most prevalent disabilities in school-age children, with an estimated 5–15% rate across languages and cultures (American Psychiatric Association, 2013). Attention Deficit Hyperactivity Disorder (ADHD) is also quite prevalent, with approximately 5% of all school-aged children being diagnosed with ADHD (American Psychiatric Association, 2013). The comorbidity of ADHD and LD is estimated to be 31–45% (DuPaul, Gormley & Laracy, 2013). Due to this high figure, and a shared continuum of symptomology, these disabilities will be discussed together.

Young people with LD and ADHD tend to have difficulties initiating and maintaining close relationships with their parents, teachers and peers (Al-Yagon, 2016). Students with ADHD have challenges with academic achievement, lower grades and scores on achievement tests and are less likely to complete high school or go to college. They experience high levels of frustration at school, and many are placed in special education programs due to comorbid LD or emotional disabilities (Wiener & Daniels, 2016).

Some of the characteristics of LD and ADHD correspond with difficulties in social, emotional and behavioural skills: information processing, and performance and production deficits (LD), attention deficits and impulsivity (ADHD).

Adolescents with LD have twice the risk of emotional distress, and girls were doubly as likely to be involved in violence or attempt suicide (Svetaz, Ireland & Blum, 2000).

Al-Yagon (2016) found that internalising behaviours (loneliness, anxiety, social withdrawal) and externalising behaviours (hyperactivity, aggression) were more prevalent in students with LD than their typically developing peers. Adolescents with comorbid LD–ADHD reported higher levels of negative affect, peer network loneliness, peer-dyadic loneliness, externalising behaviour problems and internalising behaviour problems, compared to their peers with typical development. Adolescents with comorbid LD–ADHD also manifested higher levels of negative affect compared to their peers with LD. These characteristics tend to negatively impact the relationships between students with LD and their teachers. Additionally, Gutshall (2013) found that when students have the label of learning disability, the LD label impacts teachers' perceptions and attitudes towards them, thereby affecting their relationship and the students' sense of connectedness to their school.

Adolescents with ADHD tend to be reactive rather than self-determined in their behaviour towards their environment (Wiener & Daniels, 2016). Students with ADHD often know of teachers' expectations and what needs to be done academically, but many possess poor study skills, procrastinate and have problems goal setting (Wiener & Daniels, 2016). This may leave them ill prepared to handle the shift to autonomy that comes with entering high school, especially in the areas of taking more responsibility for their learning and advocating for themselves. Low levels of personal agency may be due to the neurocognitive deficits associated with ADHD, and may cause students to be the recipients of exclusionary discipline practices.

Intellectual disabilities

Students with intellectual disabilities may possess one or more of several risk factors that can negatively impact their sense of connectedness. These include: (a) mental health problems, (b) social and economic disadvantage, (c) cognitive impairment, (d) developmental immaturity, (e) poor adaptive skills, (f) difficulties learning, (g) low social competence, (h) attention deficits and (i) problems with behaviour and self-regulation (Gilmore, Campbell, Shochet & Roberts, 2013). Blacher, Baker & Eisenhower (2009) found that students with intellectual disability (ID) who were placed in general education classes had less stable relationships with their teachers than their typically developing peers did. They cited challenging behaviour as one characteristic that negatively impacted student–teacher relationships, while social skill competency was a predictor of closer relationships. A student's cognitive ability was shown to affect his relationship with both teachers and peers.

As students with ID grow older, these factors tend to increase their negative impact on relationships. Gilmore et al. (2013) found that some students with ID also possess characteristics that make them more resilient, such as: optimism, self-efficacy, social competence, easy temperament, mastery orientation, family cohesiveness, positive school experiences. They also suggested that students with ID actually have higher levels of school connectedness than their typically developing peers. This was attributed to higher levels of support, caring relationships with adults, high expectations from adults and meaningful participation in school activities that may occur as part of the one-on-one specialised support that students with ID typically receive.

Emotional and behavioural disabilities

It is essential to children's well-being that teachers and parents teach them self-discipline, problem solving skills and responsibility for their own behaviour. When students have these skills they also have a higher quality of life. It builds their capacity for resilience, well-being and connectedness (Burgess, 2014). This is especially true for students with emotional and behavioural disabilities (EBD), as these are areas in which many students with EBD have deficits.

Students with EBD often experience many challenges within the school environment (Kern, 2015) and are often subject to exclusionary discipline practices such as suspension and expulsion due to health-risk behaviours such as substance abuse, weapon-related violence and physical violence resulting in serious bodily injury (U.S. Department of Education, 2014). Students with EBD have low school connectedness, as they struggle to develop positive relationships with their teachers as well as their peers, and often do not acquire a commitment to education (Hecker, Young & Caldarella, 2014; Morgan, 2010; Ryan, Pierce & Mooney, 2008). These issues are especially prevalent for girls, and because EBD is under identified in girls, this means that they don't often receive the supports and interventions they require (Srsic & Hess Rice, 2012). The lack of identification is due to the fact that girls typically display more internalising behaviours rather than externalising. Because these behaviours include anxiety, depression and withdrawal, they are frequently identified as having EBD in hospital settings rather than schools. The characteristics of EBD often prevent these girls from developing and sustaining lasting healthy relationships. Early intervention is important, as this difficulty can end up causing isolation.

Autism spectrum disorder

Adolescents with autism spectrum disorder (ASD) have an increased risk of mental health problems, but there is little research on prevention and intervention for this population (Shochet, Saggers, Carrington, Orr, Wurfl, Duncan & Smith, 2016). Students with ASD experience high rates of social exclusion, and their needs are often not understood or supported (Saggers et al., 2015). Shochet et al. (2016) suggest that school connectedness and resilience are the two most important interrelated protective factors for students with ASD, but some of the characteristics of ASD, such as social and communication difficulties, difficulties with changes and transitions, and low optimism and self-esteem may negatively impact those factors. In a study conducted by Saggers et al. (2015), both parents and students rated students with ASD as having a low connection to school. Other characteristics of autism that can impact relationship building and school motivation are: (a) limited verbal and nonverbal communication, (b) poor eye contact, (c) difficulty understanding body language, (d) difficulty developing and maintaining relationships, (e) restricted, repetitive behaviour such as speech, (f) unusual object use, (g) ritualised behaviour, (h) fixated interests and (i) heightened or diminished reactivity to sensory input (Shochet et al., 2016).

Humphrey and Symes (2011) posit that autism can be challenging to school connectedness for several reasons, beginning with the misperception that being academically able, as many students with high functioning autism are, means being socially able. The preference for routine, predictability and low sensory stimulation is adverse to the noisy chaos of school. In addition, students with autism may possess cognitive profiles and learning styles that challenge educators' assumptions about teaching and learning. Lastly, students with autism unfortunately experience higher incidences of bullying than their peers, which is detrimental to their relationships, social skills and mental health.

Students with ASD may have low self-esteem and be prone to depression and anxiety. This depression can put stress on parents and teachers, thus having a negative effect on the youth's supportive relationships. Young people with ASD typically lack the coping strategies necessary to manage negative mood and anxiety and cope in stressful social situations. They may rely on unhelpful strategies such as avoidance, suppression, eye contact avoidance or lashing out (Shochet et al., 2016). This may cause a lack of connectedness, as teachers often struggle with their lack of attention, emotions, social skills, behaviour and underperformance academically.

Transition to secondary school is particularly difficult for students with ASD, as it involves a larger educational environment, changing classes, more people to interact with and increasing academic demands (Strnadová, Cumming & Danker, 2016). Self and affect regulation have a reciprocal relationship with connectedness, as they lead to more positive social interactions, which leads to greater connectedness, which leads to more positive social interactions. Therefore, intervention should focus on the social and emotional needs of students with ASD as a priority to support them in being successful at school (Saggers et al., 2015).

Chronic health issues

Students who have an ongoing medical condition, disease or who are medically fragile are said to have chronic illness. Shaw and McCabe (2008, p. 74) define chronic illness as: "a medical condition of extended duration that creates impairment in adaptive behaviour and socially defined roles." In the USA, some 18% of all children are reported to have a chronic illness and 1.5% of children are unable to regularly attend school because of illness (American Academy of Pediatrics, Council on Children with Disabilities, 2005). Chronic illnesses that may limit a child's educational participation include asthma, cancer, cystic fibrosis, diabetes and traumatic brain injury.

Certain characteristics of a student's chronic illness may affect his/her ability to learn. Many students with chronic illness report that they experience difficulties in attention, memory, processing speed and cognitive deficits (Glang, Ettel, Tyler & Todis, 2012). A number of them have difficulty returning to school after their health had improved, having fallen so far behind their peers academically. School refusal is common, and homebound instruction is required for some students to allow them to catch up (Shaw and McCabe, 2008). Shaw and McCabe also suggest that a lack of academic motivation may be another issue. Chronic illnesses such as cancer, asthma, cystic fibrosis, diabetes and epilepsy may cause fatigue, lethargy, irritability and depression.

Post school outcomes differ by age group and medical condition, but Glang et al. (2012) provided evidence of poor post-high school outcomes for students with chronic illnesses across the board. School-related contributors to poor outcomes such as lack of teacher awareness, lack of hospital-school communication and poor school-family relationships were also reported. Students with chronic health issues report significantly lower feelings of school connectedness and positive feelings towards school than their healthier peers (Svavarsdottir, 2008). This is most likely due to the fact that they have low attendance rates, and many experience multiple transitions in and out of hospitals each school year. Svavarsdottir (2008) suggests that school nurses have a large role in supporting and facilitating the school connectedness of chronically ill students. It is also crucial for nurses, as well as other school staff, to foster a sense of belonging and connectedness among students with psychiatric illness, particularly to circumvent health risk behaviours.

Risk factors

The characteristics of the disabilities discussed above may contribute to the risks that adolescents face, such as mental health issues, violence, substance abuse and sexuality. Risk factors are those attributes, characteristics or exposure that increase the chances that young people will be involved with the risks above (Blum & Mmari, 2005). Poor mental health, which is a characteristic of many of the disabilities listed above, may be the most important risk factor, as there is an extensive negative correlation between mental health symptoms and school connectedness (Saggers et al., 2015). In a study conducted by Saggers et al., school connectedness predicted mental health symptoms later in life, but having mental health issues at the start did not predict level of school connectedness. They also discovered that boys tended towards more depressive symptoms, and girls displayed more anxiety symptoms.

Another risk factor, relationships with peers, teachers and family is also a protective factor (see next section). Blacher et al. (2009) posit that negative relationships early on can lead to a poor sense of self-worth, social development, attachment to adults, school engagement and poor relationships with authority figures. As students with disabilities grow older, their relationships with teachers may become more negatively impacted by their behavioural and social deficits.

Students who have less secure attachment and/or poor relationships with their parents and other family members are also at risk for mental health issues and poor school connectedness (Al-Yagon, 2016). Svetaz et al. (2000) hypothesised that child–parent relationships may be negatively affected by parental stress caused by the child's behaviour. Strong peer relationships are crucial for this group of students, as low quality friendships affect the overall adjustment of students with disabilities and receiving support from classmates is the strongest influence over preventing bullying (Al-Yagon, 2016; Humphrey & Symes, 2011).

In addition to disability and the factors listed above, other risk factors include: gender (boys experience a lower level of school connectedness than girls), race (poorer for minorities), low achievement, social and economic disadvantage, developmental immaturity, poor adaptive skills, low social competence, attention deficits and problems with behaviour and self-regulation (Blacher et al., 2009; Gilmore et al., 2013). Examining risk factors allows administrators, educators and families to address deficits in these areas. A strengths-based model allows one to do this by focusing and capitalising on protective factors, such as school connectedness, which has been identified as the single school-related factor to provide protection for adolescents (Gilmore et al., 2013).

Protective factors

Protective factors are those conditions or variables that enhance the likelihood of positive outcomes and decrease the likelihood of negative outcomes when exposed to risk (Blum & Mmari, 2005). School connectedness is the single largest education-based protective factor against mental illness and emotional distress, as for some students with disabilities, school is seen as a place of comfort, not just a source of stress (Shochet et al., 2016; Svetaz et al., 2000). School connectedness and resilience were the two important interrelated protective factors. A student's level of school connectedness is a strong predictor of well-being and positive social interactions, which lead to more positive social interactions and greater connectedness (Shochet et al., 2016). Svavarsdottir (2008) discussed the effects of positive school experiences for students with chronic illnesses; these experiences provide students with a sense of control as well as increasing their self-esteem. They can also help to strengthen peer relationships and decrease emotional stress, which are characteristics of having a disease.

Family cohesiveness is a protective factor, in that it has been shown to increase a young person's resiliency (Gilmore et al., 2013). Murray and Greenburg (2006) found that the quality of parent–child relationships can positively affect the child's functioning and social emotional adjustment. Positive communication and partnerships between schools and families are also seen as protective factors, as these increase the individual's and family's quality of life (Burgess, 2014).

Burgess (2014) purports student characteristics, such as self-discipline, problem solving skills and taking responsibility for one's own behaviour can also serve as protective factors. When students have these skills they also have a higher quality of life, as it builds their capacity for resilience, well-being and connectedness. Social competence predicts closer relationships and makes students with disabilities more resilient (Blacher et al., 2009; Gilmore et al., 2013). Other intrapersonal protective factors that increase the resiliency of students with disabilities include: easy temperament and mastery orientation (Gilmore et al., 2013).

Saggers et al. (2015) surveyed students with disabilities about what they thought were risk and protective factors for them in the school environment. The students surveyed said the following ten things were the most difficult for them:

- planning for assignments
- working as part of a group
- handwriting and being neat
- coping with change
- coping with bullying or teasing
- handwriting speed
- copying information from the board
- doing homework
- staying calm when other students annoyed them
- staying calm when the classroom is very noisy.

Students thought that technology use, being able to take breaks and having time away from others were the top three things that would help them at school. They also mentioned being told of schedule changes, being provided with copies of teacher notes, quiet spaces to work and using their own special interests to do projects as helpful. Giving students a voice about their own challenges and needs and comparing the internal and external protective factors for students with disabilities is a valuable exercise to support the design and implementation of intervention for students with disabilities and their families (Gilmore et al., 2013).

Interventions

Although different categories of disabilities exist for school-age children, they share many of the same risk and protective factors. Therefore, interventions should be designed that capitalise on the protective factors possessed by students in order to mediate the risk factors. Several strategies can be found in the research literature, along with studies that relied on students' own metacognition to make suggestions for improvement of the school experience.

Gilmore et al. (2013) suggests that interventions focus upon characteristics that have been shown to respond well to intervention, such as: self-concept, impulse control, achievement, motivation and problem solving.

Wiener and Daniels (2016) interviewed students with autism to determine what supports and interventions they felt would improve their school experience. Students thought that classrooms that minimised distractions or that captured and held their attention would support their learning best. Smaller classes, where everyone had a say and the teacher had more time to support them, were also favoured. When asked to identify positive teacher traits, students wanted teachers who were: funny or fun, warm but in control, helpful, open-minded and understanding of their disability. Students also commented that teachers were good at supporting them in the classroom, but complained about the lack of monitoring, feedback and follow up. Students preferred hands-on activities, particularly those that incorporated technology.

Taking the above suggestions into account, it would be appropriate to consider a multilayered intervention that targets schools, teachers, parents and students with disabilities and is centred around skill acquisition, functional skills and quality of life (Shochet et al., 2016). This intervention system should incorporate suggestions from the literature. Wiener and Daniels (2016) suggest that students with disabilities would benefit from interventions that specifically address their performance deficits and low levels of personal agency. These should include explicit teaching of organisational strategies for completing homework, planning and general organisational skills They also advocate for self-determination and self-advocacy skill training to increase students' independence and ownership of their learning. Assignments should be designed in a way that provides account-ability and feedback, and teachers should regularly check students' notebooks and homework.

Burgess (2014) suggests that intervention should be based on the premise that intelligence is fluid and very much influenced by environment. She emphasises the importance of teaching students to be independent thinkers and transfer the knowledge, skills and strategies to their everyday lives. She suggests that this can be accomplished by encouraging the language of thinking (summarise, estimate, conclude), and developing metacognition by teaching students to be persistent, think flexibly and question. The *Habits of Mind* approach (Costa & Kallick, 2009) provides a framework of 16 problem solving, life related skills that promote the acquisition of the skills suggested by Burgess. Previously it was thought that the *Habits of Mind* were only applicable to individuals who were already functioning at a high level, but it has been found to be effective in inclusive schooling environments (Burgess, 2014).

Interventions should also target students' social emotional needs and adaptive behaviour (Saggers et al., 2015; Shochet et al., 2016). This can be accomplished by supporting students' social and emotional well-being, implementing positive behaviour support and using a flexible approach tailored for each individual student. Evidence-based practices that are effective in these areas include social skills training and cognitive behaviour therapy (Shochet et al., 2016). To be fully effective, interventions should be part of a school-based positive mental health approach and cater for individual differences, including gender (Hossfeld & Taormina, 1998; Svavarsdottir, 2008).

Teachers, parents and peers are an important part of any intervention. Teachers need to ask students how they learn best, and be empathetic, tolerant and accepting, and peers should be taught to be empathetic and not tease fellow students for having disabilities or dislike them for their social and behavioural deficits (Wiener & Daniels, 2016). Srsic and Hess (2012) recommend that professionals working with students with disabilities receive professional development in the areas of disabilities and gender responsive programming. Home-school partnerships are important to individual and family quality of life. Schools should encourage family to be part of the decision making process for services for students with disability and collaborate like partners. Because many current "partnership" activities such as fund raising benefit the school but not the family, schools should find ways to partner that benefits families so that the partnership is authentic and reciprocal. Mindfulness training for parents can help to strengthen their relationships with their children as well as with the school (Haydicky, Wiener, Badali, Milligan & Ducharme, 2012). The best way to support parents of students with behavioural challenges is to support them in learning how to identify and use their parenting skills (Burgess, 2014).

Lastly, getting students involved in the wider school and neighbourhood community fosters connectedness. Svavarsdottir (2008) proposed that participation in extracurricular activities results in higher levels of connectedness to school. Students with interests in singular pursuits or hobbies had goals for after school and were therefore more involved in school and the community (Wiener & Daniels, 2016).

Conclusion

School connectedness may be more important to students with disabilities than any other group of students. This is because the characteristics of various disabilities may cause students to have difficulties with the social, emotional and behavioural facets of school. School connectedness has been identified as one of the greatest protective factors for this population, particularly in the areas of mental illness and emotional distress (Shochet et al., 2016; Svetaz et al., 2000). The quality of relationships with peers and adults is central to a student's sense of connectedness, and therefore needs to be a focal point of intervention, as it has been identified as both a risk and protective factor. Other important aspects of connectedness that typically impact students with disabilities on a greater level than their typically developing peers include classroom engagement, discipline policies and behaviour management.

To intervene and improve the sense of connectedness students with disabilities feel at school, risk and protective factors can be assessed. The protective factors can then be fostered and used as strengths to ameliorate the risk factors. Interventions should therefore target the fostering of qualities such as school connectedness, resilience, family cohesiveness, self-discipline, problem solving skills and taking responsibility for one's own behaviour to counter risk factors such as substance abuse, poor relationships, early onset of sexuality, violence and mental health issues.

The suggestions for interventions to improve the sense of connectedness students with disabilities feel at school are based on the literature, and include targeting performance deficits, self-determination, self-advocacy, organisational skills, the environment, social emotional skills and adaptive behaviour. This highlights the need for a multilayered holistic approach that includes input and intervention involvement of schools, teachers, parents, the community and the students themselves. Forthcoming research in the field should consider the effects of such interventions on students with disabilities specifically, in order to tailor future interventions to meet the unique needs of that population in regards to improving their sense of school connectedness.

THEORY TO PRACTICE

Suggestions can be divided into the following areas:
Teacher educators can...

- Introduce the importance of cultivating positive relationships with students with disabilities and provide supporting research at an appropriate point in the curriculum for preservice and inservice teachers, administrators, and other relevant staff
- Provide the preservice teachers with the opportunity to get to know their students and develop appropriate positive relationships with them during their fieldwork experience
- Deliver a comprehensive curriculum that includes instruction in social, emotional learning and a positive behavioural support approach to classroom management

School leaders can...

- Prioritise the use of evidence-based practices to support students with disabilities academically, socially, emotionally and behaviourally
- Encourage and support the use of scientifically sound positive discipline practices rather than punitive exclusionary practices
- Implement a school-based positive mental health approach that caters for individual differences, including gender
- Contribute to research that supports efforts in the field to improve best practices for students with disabilities
- Involve parents in ways that are beneficial to the family, and foster strong school-family communication and collaboration
- Encourage the participation of students with disabilities in the school's extracurricular activities
- Provide professional development for teachers in areas important to teaching in today's inclusive classrooms
- Provide learning opportunities for parents of students with disabilities that will support them in their parenting

Teachers can...

- Respect and respond to students' metacognitive needs, and value their interests, motivation and point of view
- Celebrate and respect diversity in their classrooms, and teach students to do the same
- Foster caring supportive relationships with all of their students
- Support active engagement for students with diverse abilities

6

STUDENT BONDING AND ATTACHMENT

School bonding and attachment

School bonding is the extent which students are able to create and maintain interpersonal relationships with staff and peers on their school campus (Ainsworth & Bowlby, 1991; Chapman et al., 2013; Hirschi, 1969). As students develop relationships, they begin to adopt the values and beliefs associated with their groups. Their group membership influences their level of commitment to school, which affects their desired personal goals and the time they allocate towards engaging in behaviour consistent with their personal goals (Bandura, 1979; Catalano & Hawkins, 1996; Catalano et al., 2004; Matsueda, 1988). Secure levels of school bonding are developed through adult support (e.g., teacher–student relationships), positive peer relationships and a commitment to education (Blum, 2005a). These domains act as a protective foundation with which a student can achieve academic and behavioural success (Ainsworth & Bowlby, 1991; Catalano & Hawkins, 1996; Catalano et al., 2004).

School attachment is the extent that a student enjoys the school experience and engages in behaviour consistent with achieving their personal goals (Libbey, 2004). School attachment includes student feelings regarding whether or not staff and their peers on their school campus like them, enjoy being at school and they contribute to the school environment. These feelings held by students impact their level of involvement in school (Catalano et al., 2004; Hirschi, 1969). Involvement refers to students engaging in behaviour consistent with their personal goals (e.g., participating in after school clubs and organisations). Similar to school bonding, a student's ability to develop secure levels of school attachment is dependent on the level of adult support, positive peer relationships and environmental factors (e.g., opportunities to participate in after school clubs and organisations) (Blum, 2005a). Students who have developed a variety of secure bonds to staff and peers on campus will have increased level of school attachment (Ainsworth & Bowlby, 1991; Bowlby, 2007; Shaver et al., 1996). These bonds, as well as the availability of after school clubs and organisations, and the student's opportunity to participate in clubs and organisations further affect their level of school attachment (Blum, 2005a; Catalano et al., 2004).

School bonding and school attachment are presented in the same chapter because of their inter-related roles in student life. Students who are able to create and maintain positive relationships with their teachers as well as their peers are more fond of school, feel that school is an important part of their life and are more likely to be more involved in school and participate in after school clubs, organisations or school sponsored events (Blum, 2005a; Catalano et al., 2004; DASH-CDC, 2009; McNeely et al., 2002). Ultimately a student's level of school bonding affects their level of school attachment. Although there is a variety of factors that effect school bonding and attachment, they can be shaped by three major areas: teacher–student relationships, peer relationships and involvement opportunities (Bucalos & Lingo, 2005; Catalano, Berglund, Ryan, Lonczak, & Hawkins, 2002; Morgan, 2010; Regan & Michaud, 2011). Each of these areas contributes to the amount of secure bonds a student creates with staff and peers on their school campus.

Teacher–student relationships

The teacher–student relationship is the foundation of the school experience. Positive teacher–student relationships are essential for classroom management, positive school experiences and academic and behavioural success (Bucalos & Lingo, 2005; Petrie, 2014; Zullig et al., 2011). Teachers who make a conscious effort to understand their students as individuals and increase the amount of positive interactions they have with their students create a safe and positive learning environment (Bucalos & Lingo, 2005; Regan & Michaud, 2011). A safe and positive learning environment promotes student engagement in class activities and assignments and, ultimately, leads to academic success (Ding & Hall, 2007; Regan & Michaud, 2011). By creating a safe learning environment, teachers can also utilise strategies and supports to integrate essential post-secondary skills (e.g., cooperation, problem solving, conflict resolution, group decision making, social skills) and recognise the positive behaviour of their students (Durlak & Weissberg, 2007; Durlak, Weissberg, Dymnicki, Taylor, & Schellinger, 2011; Regan & Michaud, 2011). Teachers can develop positive relationships with their students through the use of culturally responsive pedagogy, specific positive verbal praise and mentoring.

Culturally responsive pedagogy

Culturally Responsive Pedagogy (CRP) recognises the importance of including traits of students' cultures in all aspects of learning (Ladson-Billings, 1994). Caring teacher–student relationships are related to increasing learning outcomes for students (Baker, 1999; Toshalis, 2015). Teacher–student relationships are critical in aiding students to adapt to the expectations and demands of the school environment (Milner, 2011). Positive teacher relationships with minority students may help bridge the gap between home and school cultures (Baker, 1999; Toshalis, 2015). A breakdown in these relationships can lead to student alienation and isolation, which prohibits students from developing secure bonds (Baker, 1999; Hirschi, 1969). Safe and responsive classroom environments, where teachers create meaningful connections with their students, form a community that works together to persist through the academic and behavioural demands of school (Baker, 1999; Skiba, Michael, Nardo & Peterson, 2002). CRP offers teachers the ability to create safe learning environments for their students, whereby students are afforded the opportunity to explore different avenues of interests (Toshalis, 2015).

Culturally responsive pedagogy allows students to develop critical understanding about knowledge (Milner, 2010; Toshalis, 2015). It offers them the ability to develop a voice where multiple perspectives are allowed along with learning through discourse as well as exposes students to political and historical content that directly addresses discrimination, stereotypes, institutional racism and interpersonal prejudice (Milner, 2010; Toshalis, 2015). CRP facilitates and support achievement of all students, whereby the strengths of students are culturally supported. CRP consists of three dimensions: (a) institutional, (b) personal and (c) instructional (Richards, Brown & Forde, 2007).

Institutional CRP refers to the policies and procedures developed by administration on a school campus according to their values (Little, 1999; Richards et al., 2007). Administrative policies and procedures concern the allocation of resources to programs within the school and the ability for all students to access specialised or advanced programs (Little, 1999; Nieto, 2002). Allocation of resources can also consist of the degree a school and its accompanying programs incorporate individuals from the community. This can consist of the school providing opportunities from parents and community leaders to get involved with the school in order to further enhance the bonds created between families, students and staff (Nieto, 2002).

Personal CRP refers to the ability of the teachers to self-reflect on their attitudes and beliefs about themselves and others (Kauffman & Landrum, 2013; McKenna, 2013; Richards et al., 2007). This self-reflection includes the teachers analysing personal biases that may be held by the teacher due to their personal history, values; or beliefs (Olmeda & Kauffman, 2003; Richards et al., 2007; Villegas & Lucas, 2002). Although this may be an uncomfortable experience, teachers who are able to resolve negative biases are better able to create safe and responsive learning environments that are open and understanding (Richards et al., 2007). This can also contribute to improved teacher–student relationships where understanding personal, cultural, language and ethnic differences are valued and supported (Richards et al., 2007; Toshalis, 2015).

Building on the importance of teacher–student relationships emphasised in the personal CRP dimension, instructional CRP refers to the teaching strategies, supports and tools provided in the classroom to account for the personal, cultural, language and ethnic differences of the students in a class (Toshalis, 2015). Tools concern the ability of the classroom teacher to provide sufficient materials (e.g., text books) necessary to improve the academic outcomes of their students. Strategies and supports concern the teacher-led activities conducted in the classroom, including direct and differentiated instruction, cooperative learning arrangements, peer tutoring and visual supports (Gay, 2002; Richards et al., 2007). Schools that develop policies and procedures with the best interests of all students, employ self-reflective teachers who promote and value students' differences and utilise tools, strategies, supports to integrate those differences within the classroom are able to build positive teacher–student relationships (McKenna, 2013; Milner, 2010; Richards et al., 2007; Toshalis, 2015).

Specific positive praise

Poorly managed classrooms are unable to foster positive academic and social learning environments and detract from building meaningful relationships (Blum, 2005a). Unfortunately, many teachers struggle to create safe and positive learning environments due to their comfort ability with using proactive interventions designed to prevent problem behaviour (Heward, 2003; Walker, Ramsey & Gresham, 2003). Typically, teachers resort to more reactive means to address misbehaviour (e.g., reprimands, class removal, detention), which not only negatively reinforces problem behaviour, but also prohibits the development of positive teacher–student relationships (Cooper, Heron & Heward, 2007; Heward, 2003; Maag, 2001; Regan & Michaud, 2011). Specific positive praise contingent on appropriate student behaviour is a highly effective form of positive reinforcement and a fundamental building block for effective classroom management that can enhance the teacher–student relationship and promote academic and behavioural success (Heward, 2003; Kennedy & Jolivette, 2008; Walker et al., 2003).

Specific positive praise is a cost effective, natural and frequently available form of positive reinforcement that is often underused by teachers (Kern, 2015; Walker et al., 2003). When used effectively, specific positive praise from the teacher to the student communicates the academic and behavioural expectations of the teacher and provides the student with feedback on the successful performance of said teacher's expectations (Kennedy & Jolivette, 2008; Kern, 2015). Furthermore, specific verbal praise can be paired with any variety of tangible reinforcers or token economy system (Cooper et al., 2007).

In order to be effective, the use of specific positive praise should adhere to a set of criteria. First, praise must be specific and immediate (Kennedy & Jolivette, 2008; Andrews, Fisher, Jenson, Morgan, Reavis & Taylor 1996). Specificity and immediacy informs the student of the exact behaviours that earned them the positive praise and is paramount to increasing the future performance of those set of behaviours (Cooper et al., 2007; Heward, 2003). Second, praise must be used frequently (Andrews et al., 1996). Specific positive praise should be provided on a ratio of 4:1 in relation to reprimands or corrective feedback (Walker et al., 2003). Third, a variety of specific positive praise should be used (Andrews et al., 1996). Variety refers to the type of specific positive praise (e.g., praising for multiple behaviours) as well as variety of students (Walker et al., 2003). Teachers must be vigilant in praising not only the students who typically engage in appropriate classroom behaviour, but also those students who engage in problem behaviour when they are behaving well (Heward, 2003; Kennedy & Jolivette, 2008). Finally, specific positive praise should be enthusiastic and genuine (Andrews et al., 1996). Teaching students to obtain teacher attention through the use of specific positive praise is a highly effective strategy in improving student behaviour and the overall classroom climate (Heward, 2003). Consistent use of specific positive verbal praise leads to more frequent positive interactions between teacher and student, thereby improving the teacher–student relationship (Walker et al., 2003; Zullig et al., 2011). These improved relationships establish secure teacher–student bonds and begin to shape a student's attitudes and beliefs towards school (Catalano et al., 2004; Catalano et al., 2015).

Mentoring

Building on the use of specific positive praise in conjunction with culturally responsive pedagogy, after school programs and mentoring programs have been found to improve teacher–student relationships (Anderson-Butcher, 2010; DASH-CDC, 2009; Savitz-Romer & Jager-Hyman, 2009). These programs integrate the aspects of verbal praise and positive attention while also integrating community members and leaders with the school environment to further enhance the school experience (Anderson-Butcher, 2010; Anderson-Butcher, Lawson, Iachini, Flaspohler, Bean & Wade-Mdivanian, 2010; Crosnoe, Johnson & Elder, 2004). Traditional community-based after-school programs such as the Boys and Girls Clubs of America and the Young Men's Christian Association (YMCA) provide youth opportunities to become involved in the community and provide levels of mentoring in an alternative environment, school-based activities and mentoring (e.g., The Check and Connect program) invite the community to the school to create effective partnerships between school and community (Anderson, Christenson, Sinclair & Lehr, 2004; Anderson-Butcher & Cash, 2010; Chan, Rhodes, Howard, Lowe, Schwartz & Herrera, 2013; Kern, 2015).

At the heart of school-based mentoring programs is the development of positive relationships between teacher, student, family and community, with the goal being to proactively prevent youth from becoming disconnected from the school environment and create secure bonds in the school, community and home environment (Anderson et al., 2004; Chan et al., 2013). School-based mentoring involves the assignment of school-based mentors who act as the intermediary between the school, home and community environments (Anderson et al., 2004). Mentors act as an alternative school-based adult who can effectively develop a secure bond with youths and can provide an additional supportive and caring relationship (Anderson et al., 2004; Chan et al., 2013). The mentor can be hired staff from the community, trained school staff or teachers. The role of the mentor is to improve student academic and behavioural outcomes, as well as establish communication between families and community service agencies to further support student outcomes (Chan et al., 2013).

School-based mentoring programs have been found to develop student–teacher relationships as well as improved student behavioural and academic outcomes and overall school connectedness (Anderson-Butcher, 2010; Durlak & Weissberg, 2007). Reported improved academic outcomes include increases in school attendance, engagement in the classroom, attitude towards school and its role in their future and academic achievement (Anderson et al., 2004; Anderson-Butcher, 2010; Anderson-Butcher & Cash, 2010; Chan et al., 2013; Durlak & Weissberg, 2007). Reported improved behavioural outcomes are engagement in pro-social behaviour (e.g., interacting with peers, following school rules and expectations) and improved peer relationships (Anderson-Butcher & Cash, 2010; Chan et al., 2013; Chan et al., 2015). Students enrolled in school-based mentoring programs also reported improved school bonding, self-esteem and self-confidence, as well as improved relationships with their parents and community members (Chan et al., 2013; Durlak & Weissberg, 2007). Relationships with families and communities will be discussed further in Chapter 8.

A positive teacher–student relationship is essential to the development of secure school bonds and improved school attachment (Catalano et al., 2004; Durlak & Weissberg, 2007). Teachers can effectively improve their relationships with their students by utilising culturally responsive pedagogy within their classrooms as well as recognising the pro-social behaviours of their students during their day-to-day interactions in the classrooms (Heward, 2003; Kennedy & Jolivette, 2008; McKenna, 2013; Milner, 2010; Richards et al., 2007; Walker et al., 2003). The incorporation of after-school or school-based mentoring programs is another avenue for developing and maintaining positive teacher–student relationships, while further developing student social skills, academic skills, school attendance and self-confidence (Anderson-Butcher & Cash, 2010; Chan et al., 2013; Durlak et al., 2011; Durlak & Weissberg, 2007; Kern, 2015).

Peer relationships

In addition to positive teacher–student relationships, students who develop positive peer relationships with pro-social peer groups develop more secure bonds within the school environment, have more positive attitudes about school and engage in more frequent behaviour related to high levels of school attachment (e.g., involvement in after-school activities, completing classwork) (Blum, 2005a; Durlak & Weissberg, 2007; Hirschi, 1969; McNeely & Falci, 2004). Conversely, students who struggle to develop positive peer relationships may become involved with anti-social peer groups and engage in higher rates of health-risk behaviour (e.g., violence towards self or others, substance abuse, dropping out of school, sexual activity) (Blum, 2005a; Catalano et al., 2004; Jager, Yuen, Putnick, Hendricks & Bornstein, 2015; McNeely & Falci, 2004; Monahan, Oesterle & Hawkins, 2010). The most important dynamic that helps to address the needs of students who struggle to develop positive peer relationships is providing them with social emotional learning opportunities (Anderson-Butcher, 2010; Durlak et al., 2011).

Social and emotional learning

Incorporating social emotional learning opportunities within the classroom is one way teachers can build positive peer relationships of their students and be proactive in addressing problem behaviour. Programs designed to promote social and emotional learning have been shown to be effective in reducing student engagement in school-level problem behaviour (e.g., truancy, school violence, classroom disruption) as well as engagement in health-risk behaviour that occurs outside the boundaries of school (e.g., substance abuse, sexual activity, community violence) (Blum, 2005a; Blum & Libbey, 2004; Catalano et al., 2004; McNeely & Falci, 2004; Monahan et al., 2010). This reduction in problem behaviour improves student social status in the classroom and affords them more opportunities to engage pro-social behaviour with their peers (Fuchs, Fuchs, Mathes & Martinez, 2002). Students who struggle with developing and maintaining interpersonal relationships may require social and emotional skills training in order to effectively engage with peers and gain membership in positive peer groups (Catalano et al., 2004).

Social emotional skills training dates back to concepts first described by Baer, Wolfe and Risely (1968) when they referred to the behaviour analyst's commitment to improving behaviours that serve to enhance people's lives. Similarly, the concept of social competence has been an important factor for many years in teaching students who struggle with developing and maintaining relationships (Kavale, Mathur & Mostert, 2004). In an effort to guide the teaching of social emotional skills, the *Prepare Curriculum* and *Skillstreaming* curricula were created to aid professionals in teaching students with social deficits (Goldstein & McGinnis, 1984; Goldstein, 1988). Social emotional skills training has gained momentum as new challenges attributed to the culturally diverse backgrounds of students entering classrooms have become increasingly evident (Learning First Alliance, 2001). In order to better prepare students to become productive members of society, schools should incorporate learning opportunities that address students' social and emotional needs (Learning First Alliance, 2001).

Unfortunately, there is no single skill that students require to achieve emotional stability; rather there is a variety of skills that are necessary for a student to be considered emotionally competent. Researchers have not agreed on an exact set of skills that define a typical 'healthy student', but five essential competencies have been identified: "(a) a positive sense of self, (b) self-control, (c) decision-making skills, (d) a moral belief system and (e) pro-social connectedness" (Guerra & Bradshaw, 2008, p. 6). Research indicates that mastery of these skills leads to emotionally stable students (Durlak et al., 2011).

While the notion of incorporating social and emotional learning opportunities into the school environment is an intriguing option, implementation recommendations differ among researchers (Guerra & Bradshaw, 2008). The most popular setting for implementation is the classroom (Durlak et al., 2011). In the classroom, teachers are able to teach social emotional skills using a combination of direct instruction, modeling, practice and feedback (Durlak et al., 2011; Sugai & Horner, 2001; Morgan, 2010). This system of implementation has resulted in student acquisition and mastery of a variety of social emotional skills (Durlak et al., 2011; Gresham et al., 2001; Morgan, 2010).

Building positive peer relationships is another component that is foundational for developing secure student bonds, but it will not remedy their difficulties in building their own relationships. Social emotional learning is an essential component that should be considered as necessary in improving peer relationships as well as levels of school bonding and attachment (Gresham et al., 2001; Morgan, 2010). When used in the context of the classroom, effective social and emotional teaching strategies offer students the opportunity to practise and master social and emotional skills while simultaneously developing positive peer relationships (Durlak et al., 2011; Gresham et al., 2001; Kavale et al., 2004; Morgan, 2010).

Involvement opportunities

While the development of positive teacher–student and peer relationships are important factors for developing student levels of school bonding and improved attitudes and beliefs towards school, which is an aspect of school attachment, they only promote a student's relationships with the school environment and may not address a student's individual goals for their future (Catalano & Hawkins, 1996; Chapman et al., 2013). A by-product of secure bonds and positive attitudes towards school is highly driven and future oriented students, who may require opportunities to engage in after-school activities and programs that can help build their personal goals for the future (Anderson-Butcher, 2010; Walsh, Ozaeta & Wright, 2010). After-school activities and programs can provide experiences that promote psychical activity, personal as well as career development and can become an important factor further developing teacher–student and peer relationships (Anderson-Butcher, 2010; Walsh et al., 2010). In order to support high levels of school attachment, schools should engage with teachers and community members to develop a variety of extracurricular after-school activities (McNeely et al., 2002; Monahan et al., 2010).

School bonding and students with disabilities

Students who are able to create and maintain positive relationships with their teachers and peers at school are more likely to adjust to the school social environment and display less challenging behaviour in the classroom and on school campuses (Loukas, Suzuki & Horton, 2006). The current research in special education indicates that students with disabilities struggle to develop positive relationships with teachers and peers (Freeman, Eber, Anderson, Irvin, Horner, Bounds & Dunlap, 2006; Milsom, 2006; Murray & Greenberg, 2001; Vincent, Horner & Sugai, 2002). This is a serious concern, as social difficulties can affect the academic and behavioural success of students with disabilities (Bryan, Burstein & Ergul, 2004; Freeman et al., 2006; Lane, Carter, Pierson & Glaeser, 2006; Murray & Greenberg, 2001).

Students with disabilities are often educated in pull-out programs or self-contained classrooms, resulting in fewer opportunities to make connections with a variety of teachers and same-age peers, resulting in fewer bonds created with others (Murray & Greenberg, 2001). They may also lack the social competencies necessary to develop and maintain positive relationships, which can lead to social isolation, alienation and the development of mental health issues (DASH-CDC, 2009; Freeman et al., 2006; Lane et al., 2006; Murray & Greenberg, 2001; Vincent et al., 2002). Difficulties with social competencies also have the potential to increase the amount of negative interactions students with disabilities experience with teachers and peers in the classroom, resulting in more frequent disciplinary actions requiring removal from the classroom and school, further isolating them (Evans & Lester, 2012; Murray & Greenberg, 2001).

Therefore culturally responsive pedagogy, specific positive praise, mentoring and involvement opportunities and social emotional learning opportunities should be incorporated into programs for students with disabilities in order to enhance the bonds they create with their teachers and peers (Anderson-Butcher, 2010; Durlak & Weissberg, 2007; Freeman et al., 2006; Heward, 2003; Lane et al., 2006; McKenna, 2013; Milner, 2010; Murray & Greenberg, 2001; Toshalis, 2015). These are essential aspects of the development of their school bonding. The lack of opportunities to create and maintain friendships may lead to decreased satisfaction with school, dropping out of school and engagement in health-risk behaviour (Bearman & Moody, 2004; Eriksson et al., 2007; Murray & Greenberg, 2001; Reschly & Christensen, 2006).

School attachment and students with disabilities

Positive secure bonds created with teachers and classmates create a sense of belonging to a school (Loukas et al., 2006). Because students with disabilities struggle to create secure bonds in school, they may have more negative attitudes towards school, resulting in less school involvement and less opportunities to participate in after-school clubs, activities, and organisations (Brigharm, Morocco, Clay & Zigmond, 2006; Eriksson, Welander & Granlund, 2007; Lane et al., 2006; Spooner, Dymond, Smith & Kennedy, 2006). Students with disabilities, unlike their general education peers, may also have limited access to after-school clubs, activities and organisations (Brigharm et al., 2006; Eriksson et al., 2007). This may be due to the limited number of staff available to support students with disabilities during after-school programming, transportation issues and skills and abilities required to participate (Brigharm et al., 2006; Eriksson et al., 2007). These can be significant barriers to improving the levels of school attachment of students with disabilities, as these students may become less attached simply due to the fact that they have a disability and are not afforded the same opportunities to participate in extra-curricular school programs as their general education peers. This in turn may affect their satisfaction with school, their attitude towards school and their academic and behavioural outcomes (Brigharm et al., 2006; Eriksson et al., 2007; Loukas et al., 2006; Spooner et al., 2006).

Improving student bonding and attachment

In order for educators to improve levels of bonding and attachment, they must first realise that they are the primary vehicles for change. The first step is making small changes to their day-to-day interactions with their students in order to develop meaningful positive relationships with them (Bucalos & Lingo, 2005). Positive relationships can be built through high incidences of positive interactions, including providing task assistance, rapport-based communication either before or after class, and providing specific positive praise for student compliance to simple requests (Kennedy & Jolivette, 2008). See Table 6.1 for examples of specific positive verbal feedback.

Educators continue to underestimate the importance of developing rapport with their students, but research has shown increased outcomes in both behaviour and

TABLE 6.1 Examples of specific positive verbal feedback

Student behaviour	Teacher feedback
Student arrives to class on time.	"It was so great to have you in class on time today!"
Student ignored another student's inappropriate behaviours.	"Awesome job ignoring today. I know it's really tough to work when other students are talking."
Student turns in homework.	"Thanks so much for turning in your homework today!"
Student raises hand and participates during instruction.	"Your hand raising was outstanding today and it was great to hear your ideas about today's lesson!"
Student assists another student in finding a new classroom.	"Thank you so much for helping Joe find his class today. He was worried and you really calmed his nerves."
Student sits and participates in a class-learning group.	"Wow! You offered some great ideas to your work group and you continued working with your group even though they didn't use all of your ideas!"
Student reads aloud in class.	"Excellent reading out-loud today! I know it was really hard to read in front of your classmates."

academics for all students as a result of effective rapport building (Heward, 2003; Kennedy & Jolivette, 2008; Kern, 2015).

Teachers should also consider the incorporation of culturally responsive pedagogy within their classrooms. One way to incorporate culturally responsive pedagogy in the classroom is developing opportunities for students to learn about their cultural heritage (Toshalis, 2015). This can be done by incorporating classroom activities that represent differing cultural histories and background including student reports, visits from community leaders and celebrations of cultural groups' achievements and contributions (Milner, 2010; Toshalis, 2015). Another simple way to incorporate culturally responsive pedagogy is to encourage discourse in the classroom (Milner, 2010). Discourse encourages students to learn from one another and understand that their backgrounds and experiences are important assets in their future success (Milner, 2010).

In addition, teachers may embed social emotional learning opportunities within the context of their academic lessons. This can be accomplished through direct instruction or peer learning opportunities. Jones, Brown, Hoglund and Aber (2010) embedded social and emotional learning within the context of early literature by incorporating reading and class discussion regarding listening, anger, assertiveness, cooperation, negotiation, mediation, understanding differences and bias. Incorporating peer tutoring programs or cooperative learning opportunities also can effectively develop student's social and emotional skills as well as provide them the opportunity to practise and master newly developed skills (Fuchs et al., 2002).

Schools should consider developing mentoring and increased access to after-school activities and programs. Durlak and Weissberg (2007) recommend that an effective extracurricular after-school programs must be: (a) related to the values of the local community, (b) matter to the students involved, (c) goal oriented and (d) explicit. It is important that schools refrain from the top down approach to developing extracurricular after-school programs, as their goals may not accurately reflect the goals of the local community (Durlak & Weissberg, 2007; Toshalis, 2015). Families and community members should be involved in the planning as well as the implementation of extracurricular after-school activities and programs (Durlak & Weissberg, 2007; Toshalis, 2015). Furthermore, if these activities and programs are not in line with what the students of the school deem to be important and relevant to their lives, they are likely to be under-attended (Anderson-Butcher, 2010). Goal-oriented activities and programs offer skill development and monitoring as they guide students towards personal growth (Durlak & Weissberg, 2007). Goal-oriented activities and programs can establish student-desired outcomes and effectively monitor student progress towards the achievement of their personal goals (Durlak & Weissberg, 2007). In order for these activities to be successful, goals set forth must be explicit and attainable (Durlak & Weissberg, 2007). In other words, personal goals must consist of observable and measureable behaviour that students can actively engage in on a daily basis to determine their progress towards their goal (Durlak & Weissberg, 2007; Heward, 2003).

Conclusion

School bonding and attachment are important domains of school connectedness. The development of positive relationships is fundamental to school connectedness. Students who develop positive relationships to their teachers and peers also become more involved in school further developing their sense of connectedness to their school. The frameworks and research presented in this chapter highlight two types of relationships that can be built in order to develop levels of school bonding as well as the development of goal-oriented after-school activities and programs that can assist in the development of student levels of school attachment. While the importance of bonding and attachment has been highlighted in this chapter, they, like the other domains of school connectedness, are often not highlighted in the development of teacher preparation programs.

THEORY TO PRACTICE

Suggestions can be divided into four areas:
   Policymakers can...

- Recognise the connection between bonding, attachment and academic and behavioural success
- Create national, state and local policies regarding access to after-school based activities and programs for all students
- Provide funding for state level teacher training in effective strategies to improve student bonding and attachment

   Teacher educators can...

- Introduce school bonding and supporting research in the curriculum for preservice and inservice teachers, administrators and other relevant staff
- Introduce school attachment and supporting research in the curriculum for preservice and inservice teachers, administrators and other relevant staff
- Provide preservice teachers with the opportunity to self-reflect on personal biases and beliefs that may inhibit development of positive teacher–student relationships
- Develop a comprehensive curriculum that includes culturally responsive pedagogy, social and emotional learning, praise and mentoring practices that can be used in conjunction with academics

   School leaders can...

- Be aware of evidence-based practices to develop levels of school bonding
- Encourage the use of evidence-based strategies to develop positive teacher–student relationships

---

- Encourage the use of evidence-based strategies to develop positive peer relationships
- Work with community leaders to establish school-based and community-based after-school programs designed to meet student goals
- Provide a variety of after-school programs that can be accessed by any member of the student body

Teachers can....

- Utilise positive interactions (e.g., positive praise, non-contingent praise, positive attention for task completion) in the classroom environment
- Establish classroom expectations that are high, fair and clearly communicated
- Encourage and facilitate discourse of differing viewpoints within the classroom
- Plan for flexibility within the class schedule to allow for teachable moments and personalised teacher attention
- Utilise social emotional learning activities to develop problem-solving skills, decision-making skills, positive sense of self and pro-social skills
- Incorporate opportunities to utilise pro-social skills through peer tutoring, classroom discussions or classroom leadership roles
- Develop after school programs for students to learn or enhance extracurricular skills including clubs, sports, tutoring and community volunteer opportunities

7

STUDENT ENGAGEMENT

School engagement

School engagement refers to the degree to which a student engages in school-related behaviours (Catalano et al., 2004; Farrington et al., 2012; Jimerson, Campos & Greif, 2003). School-related behaviours consist of academic behaviours and behaviours consistent with setting goals and deferring gratification, which is also referred to as perseverance (Farrington et al., 2012; Jimerson et al., 2003). School engagement is the application of behaviours related to a student's level of involvement in school (Catalano et al., 2004). Students with higher levels of school engagement display higher levels of commitment to their education by frequently engaging in school-related behaviours in order to achieve their academic and post-secondary goals (Farrington et al., 2012; Gottfredson & Hirschi, 1990; Jimerson et al., 2003; Sorenson & Brownfield, 1995). A student's ability to defer gratification to achieve an ultimate goal will affect their level of school engagement (Catalano et al., 2004; & Hirschi, 1990; Sorenson & Brownfield, 1995).

School engagement can be broken down into two constructs, academic behaviour and academic perseverance (Farrington et al., 2012). Students who are successful at both typically participate in academic activities within the classroom, participate in school-related activities, enjoy school activities and engage in behaviour consistent with their beliefs and perceptions about the social context of school (Furlong, Whipple, St. Jean, Simental, Soliz & Punthuna, 2003; Jimerson et al., 2003). The micro-description of school engagement involves behaviours within the classroom (e.g., turning in homework, completing class assignments, being organised), beliefs and perceptions used to problem solve and social skills used to develop relationships with peers and adults (Farrington et al., 2012). Thus, school engagement is considered to be one of the four components required to build school connectedness (DASH-CDC, 2009).

Academic behaviours

Often thought of as classic school expected behaviour, academic behaviours are observable evidence that a student is engaged in learning, and consist of: (a) attending school, (b) arriving to class on time, (c) completing class work, (d) completing homework, (e) studying, (f) regularly turning in assignments, (g) participating in classroom discussion and activities, (h) going to class, doing homework, (i) organising materials, (j) participating and (k) studying (Farrington et al., 2012). Academic perseverance works through academic behaviour, as academic behaviours are the outcome of students who are able to set and achieve short-term and long-term goals (Farrington et al., 2012).

Attending school is considered the most important academic behaviour (Allensworth & Easton, 2007). Students who do not regularly attend class miss out on regular academic instruction and struggle to consistently complete classwork and homework, which affects their grades, test scores and overall school experience (Allensworth & Easton, 2007; Farrington et al., 2012). Because of this outcome, there has been a growing body of research advocating for revising harsh exclusionary discipline policies (e.g., suspension, expulsion), which serve to further remove students who already struggle with consistently attending school and engaging in academic behaviour (Evans & Lester, 2010). Poor school attendance is also a typical characteristic of students who have lower levels of school connectedness and can contribute to engagement in health-risk behaviour beyond the boundaries of the school (Blum, 2005a).

While attending school is an important factor of school engagement, spending time engaged in school work outside of the classroom is also an important factor of school engagement (Cooper, Robinson & Patall, 2006; Credé & Kuncel, 2008; Keith, Diamond-Hallam & Fine, 2004). School work outside of the classroom consists of study skills, study habits and homework. Study skills are the strategies students use in order to develop their knowledge and master content, while study habits refer to the student's ability to set aside time and organise materials for the purpose of studying (Credé & Kuncel, 2008; Farrington et al., 2012). Regularly completing homework outside of school is a consistent trait of students who also engage in high rates of study habits and independent practice and is shown to have a greater impact on student achievement overall than completing homework in school (Cooper et al., 2006; Keith et al., 2004).

While engagement in academic behaviours is not only indicative of students with high levels of school engagement and improved academic outcomes, it can also contribute to the development of high levels of school bonding and attachment (Blum, 2005a; DASH-CDC, 2009). Students who regularly attend school, participate in class and complete their work often develop stronger teacher–student relationships and positive peer relationships to pro-social peer groups and become more involved in school activities and programs (Catalano et al., 2004; Durlak & Weissberg, 2007; Farrington et al., 2012; Walker et al., 2003).

Academic perseverance

Farrington et al. (2012) defined academic perseverance as the quality, intensity and duration with which a student engages in academic behaviour. Researchers have used terms such as grit, tenacity, delayed gratification, self-discipline and self-control to describe students who demonstrate high levels of academic perseverance (Duckworth, Peterson, Matthews & Kelly, 2007; Gottfredson & Hirschi, 1990; Sorenson & Brownfield, 1995). Perseverance requires that students stay focused on their goals despite obstacles, and ignore short-term distractions or temptations that may take them off of their desired course (Duckworth et al., 2007). These students are able to prioritise long-term goal attainment over short-term pleasures (Farrington et al., 2012; Gottfredson & Hirschi, 1990; Sorenson & Brownfield, 1995). Students who engage in academic behaviours more frequently, for longer periods of time, and with a directed course of action are able to effectively master content (Duckworth et al., 2007; Farrington et al., 2012).

Another defining characteristic of academic perseverance is a student's ability to deal with setbacks. While engaging in academic behaviour frequently and intensely is not a guaranteed predictor of success, when students with high levels of academic perseverance experience failure, they continue to stay the course and refrain from revising their long-term goals (Duckworth et al., 2007; Farrington et al., 2012). This ability to learn from failure is indicative of a student's ability to defer gratification in order to achieve a more meaningful long-term goal (Duckworth et al., 2007; Gottfredson & Hirschi, 1990).

School engagement is an important factor of student life and an integral component of school connectedness. Students who are able to consistently engage in academic behaviours and persevere through failure and short-term distractions are more likely to develop a commitment to their education and adopt positive attitudes and beliefs about school and engage in pro-social behaviour (Blum, 2005a; Catalano et al., 2004; CDC, 2009; McNeely et al., 2002). Self-control is the major factor that effects school engagement and contributes to a student's ability to engage in academic behaviour and academic perseverance (Duckworth et al., 2007; Farrington et al., 2012).

Self-control

As defined in Chapter 2, self-control theory refers to an individual's ability to defer gratification, with those individuals who lack self-control more likely to engage in behaviour that results in immediate gratification (Gottfredson & Hirschi, 1990; Sorenson & Brownfield, 1995). In conjunction with social control theory and the social development model, individuals with low self-control will struggle with the involvement domain, as engaging in behaviours in order to pursue an ultimate goal requires significant delays in gratification (Catalano et al., 2004; Chapman et al., 2013; Gottfredson & Hirschi, 1990; Hirschi, 1969; Matsueda, 1988).

Gottfredson and Hirschi (1990) theorised that individuals who lack self-control often struggle with engagement in academics, as the cognitive demand is too great, and the benefits of engaging in academic tasks and activities is often more pro-longed than immediate. Although this may be the case, this deficit of self-control may not necessarily be due to cognitive disability, but rather cognitive organisation. Students who engage in self-control are able to effectively manage their own behaviour according in line with their set long-term and short-term goals (Farrington et al., 2012; Sorenson & Brownfield, 1995). Self-management and goal setting are the two primary factors that contribute to effective self-control.

Self-management

Self-management is the continuous metacognitive practice of self-assessment and evaluation (Carter, Lane, Crnobori, Bruhn & Oakes, 2011; Menzies, Lane & Lee, 2009). Cooper, Heron and Heward (2007) defined self-management as "a personal application of behaviour change tactics" (p. 578) while Lovitt (1973) maintained that self-management is one of the most important aspects of the educational system as the goal is to train students to become self-sufficient individuals. In order for students to achieve any semblance of success within the context of school or outside the boundaries of school, they must be able to successfully manage their own behaviour (Alberto & Troutman, 2013; Cooper et al., 2007; Kauffman & Landrum, 2013).

Students who struggle to manage, self-reflect or change their own behaviour will have difficulty with academic perseverance, which can result in less frequent engagement in academic behaviours (Farrington et al., 2012; Menzies et al., 2009). Self-management enables students to assess and plan their own performance in regards to their academic and behavioural success (Carter et al., 2011). In order for students to be able to successfully manage and direct their own behaviour, they must be able to engage in metacognitive practices (Cooper et al, 2007; Menzies et al., 2009).

Metacognition is essentially thinking about thinking. Students who are able to persevere through failure and continue to stay the course are able to reflect on their behaviour, address the flaws in their behaviour and address those flaws by making changes (Cooper et al., 2007; Menzies, 2009). Skills attributed to students who engage in metacognitive practices include planning, problem solving and progress monitoring (Fitzpatrick & Knowlton, 2009; Menzies et al., 2009). Unfortunately, students who struggle in school may also struggle with self-management as they may have limited skills to draw from in order to change their behaviour (Alberto & Troutman, 2013; Menzies et al., 2009).

In line with Lovitt's (1973) description of important practices in education, self-management is a skill that should be incorporated in curriculum planning in order to improve student academic perseverance and engagement in academic behaviours. Instruction in self-management strategies such as self-monitoring, self-evaluation and self-instruction are evidence-based practices designed to train students to assess and direct their own behaviour (Alberto & Troutman, 2013; Carter et al., 2011; Cooper et al., 2007; Fitzpatrick & Knowlton, 2009). The incorporation of goal setting into self-management strategies is an effective way to improve student self-control as well as school engagement. See the 'Theory to practice' section of this chapter for further detail on the implementation of these strategies.

Goal setting

While self-management refers to the extent that a student is able to assess and direct his or her own behaviour, it can become difficult if there is no pre-determined goal to direct that behaviour. Goal setting refers to a student's ability to pre-determine a desired academic or social outcome and engage in behaviour in line with achieving that predetermined goal (Catalano et al., 2004; Duckworth, Grant, Loew, Oettingen & Gollwitzer, 2011; Eccles & Wigfield, 2002). Essentially, goal setting is the bridge between perseverance and outcomes, as it acts as the motivation to engage in self-management strategies and academic behaviours (Duckworth et al., 2011; Eccles & Wigfield, 2002). Goal setting behaviour extends beyond the boundaries of school as it is linked to post-secondary outcomes including academic achievement in higher education and acquiring and maintain employment (Benitez, Lattimore & Wehmeyer, 2005; Farrington et al., 2012).

Lovitt's (1973) description of the purpose of education as developing students to become individuals highlights the importance of goal setting within the classroom. While goal setting is an evidence-based practice, it requires the incorporation of self-management strategies in order to be truly effective (Menzies et al., 2009). Students who are able to manage their own behaviour but with no desired out-come will still struggle in school, however they can be taught to set achievable short-term and long-term goals to build perseverance (Duckworth et al., 2011). Goal setting in conjunction with self-management strategies is effective in approv-ing academic perseverance, engagement in academic behaviour, and develop school engagement (Alberto & Troutman, 2013; Carter et al., 2011; Duckworth et al., 2011; Menzies et al., 2009).

School engagement and students with disabilities

Students with high levels of engagement are able to participate in cognitively challenging activities within the classroom leading to academic development and success (Farrington et al., 2012; Marks, 2000). Unfortunately, students with low levels of engagement, or who become disengaged from school, struggle to partici-pate in classroom activities and on assignments, which may lead to engagement in maladaptive behaviour resulting in removal from the classroom or school campus (Evans & Lester, 2010; Marks, 2000). Recent research in special education has found that children/youth with disabilities have difficulties performing academi-cally at high levels with consistency and are at-risk of becoming disengaged, as well as experience a lower quality of relationships with teachers and peers due to engagement in problem behaviour (U.S. Department of Education, 2016). This may be due to the fact that engagement requires students to maintain attention, engage in behavioural participation within class and show effort in the completion of academic tasks. (Klem & Connell, 2004; Marks, 2000). To combat this, special education research has focused on the development of instructional practices and interventions to enhance the school engagement of students with disabilities as well as their connectedness to their educational environments (Lane et al., 2006; Spooner et al., 2006; Wakeman, Karvonen & Ahumada, 2013).

As the rates of students with disabilities being educated in the general education classroom is increasing, improving their level of engagement is of vital importance. Academic and social deficits are prevalent characteristics of students with disabilities that impact their school engagement as well as their ability to successfully integrate into the school environment (Doren, Murray & Gau, 2014; Lane et al., 2006; Reschly & Christenson, 2006; Ryan, Pierce & Mooney, 2008; U.S. Department of Education, 2016). Although students with disabilities often have difficulty with school engagement, those who are able to engage in academic behaviours (e.g., complete homework, regularly attend class, bring materials to class) are more likely to finish school (Reschly & Christenson, 2006). If not addressed, students with disabilities may struggle to attain academic mastery, be removed from school due to harsh discipline policies or drop out (Doren et al., 2014; Evans & Lester, 2010).

Recent research indicates that programs and interventions that support the development of self-management skills and goal setting are effective in improving students' with disabilities level of engagement (Carter et al., 2011; Menzies et al., 2009). These programs and interventions further enhance these students' school engagement when combined with access to the general education curriculum as well as instruction in the general education environment with the implementation of appropriate accommodations and modifications (Carter et al., 2011; Doren et al., 2014; Marks, 2000; Murray & Greenberg, 2001). In addition, the provision of specific positive verbal feedback within the classroom as well as school reforms addressing school discipline policies also have been shown to increase the school engagement of these children/youth (Kauffman & Landrum, 2013; Kennedy & Jolivette, 2008; Regan & Michaud, 2011; Ryan et al., 2008; Vincent et al., 2002; U.S. Department of Education, 2016). The incorporation of these class-wide and school-wide programs, strategies and supports has the ability to promote lasting impacts for students with disabilities in their school engagement and beyond the boundaries of the school walls.

Improving student engagement

When considering interventions to improve student engagement, teachers should first consider strategies for improving student engagement that can be incorporated during instruction or independent practice times (Berry, 2006; Ryan et al., 2008). During instruction, incorporating discourse and opportunities for students to respond can increase student engagement which can be done by developing a series of questions or class discussion opportunities during direct instruction (Berry,

2006). When used in conjunction with specific positive verbal feedback, creating opportunities to respond is effective in improving student engagement (Berry, 2006; Kennedy & Jolivette, 2008).

Following instruction, teachers also may utilise strategies to improve student engagement during independent practice. Peer tutoring, class-wide or individual, and cooperative learning opportunities are two effective strategies in building student engagement (Fuchs et al., 2002; Ryan et al., 2008). Class-wide peer tutoring consists of the entire class participating in peer tutoring. Students are paired and engage in reciprocal teaching for the duration of the activity (Ryan et al., 2008). Peer assisted learning strategies (PALS) is another form of class-wide peer tutoring targeting specific skills where students are assigned tutor and tutee roles (Fuchs et al., 2002). While peer tutoring involves assigning student roles as tutor or tutee, cooperative learning arrangements are structured so that grouped students learn together. Students can be grouped in groups of four or five, where each student is assigned a role and responsibility (e.g., researcher, scribe, expert) (Box & Little, 2003). Group members work together to complete assignments designed to incorporate group discussion and problem-solving skills (Box & Little, 2003). Incorporating these strategies within daily classroom routines and activities can boost engagement of all student, however some students who have difficulty to self-manage their own behaviour, may require further intervention.

Self-monitoring

Self-monitoring, sometimes referred to as self-recording, refers to a student observing and recording his or her own behaviour (Alberto & Troutman, 2013; Cooper et al., 2007; Fitzpatrick & Knowlton, 2009). Self-monitoring is a popular intervention that is used to increase student engagement in academic behaviours. The first step to implementing a self-monitoring program is to select and define a target behaviour or behaviours that the student will record (e.g., arriving to class on time, turning in homework/classwork, completing problems during independent work time) (Menzies et al., 2009). The student then self-records each occurrence of the behaviour, usually on a pre-selected data sheet (see Table 7.1) (Alberto & Troutman, 2013; Cooper et al., 2007). This procedure can be paired with other classroom contingencies to improve student engagement.

Alberto and Troutman (2013) recommend that the teacher and student select an acceptable frequency of the target behaviour and collect self-monitoring data simultaneously and compare data at the end of each specific interval (e.g., end of class period, 15 minute intervals). If the student's data matches the teacher's data, students may earn access to predetermined reinforcement activities or items (Menzies et al., 2009). Once the student is successful and accurate at recording their own behaviour, the simultaneous teacher data collection procedures are faded (Cooper et al., 2007). In some cases, the simple act of self-recording behaviour serves as a behaviour change agent, but an added reinforcement contingency may be a required factor in creating the behaviour change (Cooper et al., 2007). Following

TABLE 7.1 Self-monitoring checklist with teacher verification column for independent practice activities during English language arts class period

Behaviour	Check	Teacher initials
Arrive to class and be in seat before bell rings		
Begin DO NOW activity		
Finish DO NOW activity		
Read instructions to assignment		
Answer three or more questions		
Put work into "Finished" basket		

these procedures, teachers have effectively improved student completion of independent seatwork, homework completion, hand raising and student attendance (Fitzpatrick & Knowlton, 2009). As a foundational self-management intervention, self-monitoring is effective in improving student engagement in academic behaviours, however it is simply recording occurrences of behaviour; self-evaluation builds on this and utilises goal setting to further improve student engagement.

Self-evaluation

Self-evaluation, while similar to self-monitoring, includes a set criterion, or goal, to be achieved by the student. When self-evaluating, the student continues to monitor his or her own behaviour according to criteria set by the teacher or a collaborative agreement set by the teacher and the student (see Table 7.2) (Menzies et al., 2009).

The set criteria can serve to increase appropriate behaviours (e.g., frequency of hand raising, number of problems completed, accuracy of problems completed,

TABLE 7.2 Self-evaluation checklist for independent math activity

Behaviour goal	Check
Name on paper	
Date on paper	
Complete ten or more problems	
Use regrouping strategy on all problems	
Work quietly for ten minutes or more	
Put work in "done" folder	

duration of time in seat) or to decrease problem behaviours (e.g., frequency of talk outs, frequency out-of-seat, frequency requests to leave classroom). Essentially, self-evaluation is the combination of self-monitoring procedures and goal setting. Rather than select an acceptable frequency or duration of a target behaviour, -teachers and students set goals to increase or decrease behaviours depending on the behaviour being targeted (Alberto & Troutman, 2013).

Self-evaluation procedures are similar to self-monitoring procedures. Once the teacher and student establish a target behaviour, goal and reinforcement, both the teacher and the student collect data and evaluate student performance and the end of a predetermined interval (Menzies et al., 2009). If the student's performance meets or exceeds the frequency of the durational goal, the student is able to access the pre-determined reinforcement item or activity (Cooper et al., 2007). As the student's accuracy of recording is established, the teacher recording procedures are faded. Once a student is consistently successful, the teacher and the student can meet and update the criterion to further improve student performance (Cooper et al., 2007). Self-evaluation is an effective intervention for improving academic behaviours as well as academic perseverance as students are able to work with their teacher and learn to set goals, reflect on their behaviour and set new goals based on their previous performances (Alberto & Troutman, 2013; Farrington et al., 2012).

Self-instruction

Self-instruction consists of the student using a series of self-administered verbal prompts in order to complete a task (Alberto & Troutman, 2013). These verbal prompts are an effective way for students to organise their thinking to successfully complete tasks that consist of multiple steps (Fitzpatrick & Knowlton, 2009). To teach students to use self-instruction, the teacher models the steps of a task and while saying the steps out loud; this assists the student in organising their own thinking (Alberto & Troutman, 2013; Fitzpatrick & Knowlton, 2009). The student then engages in the task matching the model's behaviour, as well as stating the steps of the task aloud with the guidance of the model. Students then apply the procedure to specific tasks within the classroom. As students become successful, and are able to follow the steps without specifically saying each one aloud, the verbal steps become covert (Alberto & Troutman, 2013; Fitzpatrick & Knowlton, 2009).

Self-instruction is an effective intervention for improving academic behaviours and academic perseverance. Students who successfully employ self-instruction are able to organise their thoughts, follow a series of steps to solve problems, and engage in a plan of attack for completing assignments, projects, group activities, or obtaining help in the classroom. Self-instruction has been effective in improving student engagement as well as their academic and behavioural outcomes (Fitzpatrick & Knowlton, 2009). To enhance the intervention's effectiveness, self-monitoring or self-evaluation procedures can be used in conjunction with self-instruction (Menzies et al., 2009).

Self-determined learning model of instruction

In order to assist teachers in supporting students who struggle with self-guided learning, Mithaug, Wehmeyer, Agran, Martin and Palmer (1998) developed the Self-Determined Learning Model of Instruction (SDLMI). This model of instruction is designed to assist students in making decisions about their interests and needs, set goals, evaluate their behavioural performance as it relates to attaining their goals and adjust their goals and behaviour in order to meet their future expectations (Wehmeyer, Palmer, Agran, Mithaug & Martin, 2000). The SDLMI consists of three phases: (a) set a goal, (b) take action and (c) adjust goal or plan (Wehmeyer et al., 2000). In each phase, students work with their teachers to address a series of questions in order to monitor their current performance in conjunction with their goals and make changes if necessary (Benitez et al., 2005). A series of teacher-objectives are also included in the SDLMI that act as a guide to assisting teachers utilising strategies and activities for assisting students in each phase of the process (Wehmeyer et al., 2000). As an intervention, the SDLMI has been effective in improving academic behaviours, academic perseverance and goal attainment for many adolescents, including adolescents with disabilities (Benitez et al., 2005; Wehmeyer et al., 2000).

Conclusion

School engagement is an important domain of school connectedness. The development of both academic behaviours and academic perseverance are fundamental to school connectedness. Students who are able to consistently engage in academic behaviours within the classroom, evaluate their performances in relation to their academic successes and failures and are able to makes changes to their behaviour in order to achieve their goals develop a commitment to education and become connected to their school. The research presented in this chapter highlights the necessary student skills required for high levels of school engagement. While these skills are important, many students struggle to manage their own behaviour. In order to improve these student's skills, a variety of self-management interventions can be used to improve their ability to evaluate and manage their own behaviour and improve their overall levels of engagement in school. While the use direct instruction and peer-based strategies to improve engagement are popular in education, they, along with self-management strategies, are often not highlighted in the development of teacher preparation programs.

THEORY TO PRACTICE

Suggestions can be divided into four areas:
  Policymakers can...

- Recognise the connection between engagement and academic and behavioural success

- Provide funding for state level teacher training in effective student engagement strategies

Teacher educators can...

- Introduce school engagement and supporting research in the curriculum for preservice and inservice teachers, administrators and relevant staff
- Develop curriculum that includes self-management and goal setting activities in conjunction with academic activities

School leaders can...

- Be aware of evidence-based strategies to develop school engagement
- Encourage the use of evidence-based strategies to develop student self-management skills
- Encourage the use of evidence-based strategies to develop student goal setting skills
- Encourage the use peer-based activities to improve student engagement
- Encourage the teacher to develop student opportunities to respond during direct instruction

Teachers can...

- Teach students self-management strategies
- Engage in academic goal-setting with students and have them track their progress
- Teach and reinforce student's academic behaviours to improve their academic success
- Develop a series of questions or discussion points during direct instruction to increase student opportunities to respond
- Develop independent practice activities requiring peer-tutoring or cooperative learning arrangements
- Employ positive interactions to further enhance student engagement

8

ENLISTING PARENTS AS PARTNERS IN THE SCHOOL CONNECTEDNESS PARADIGM

Professional organisations and researchers have supported parental involvement in the education of their children for over 100 years (Office for Standards in Education, Children's Services and Skills, 2009; Padak & Rasinski, 2010). This involvement has been discussed in the literature as parental involvement (Kroth & Edge, 2007), parent-professional partnerships (Epstein, 2005; Epstein & Sanders, 2006; Murray & Curran, 2008; Summers, Hoffman, Marquis, Turnbull, Poston & Nelson, 2005), teacher–parent collaboration (Comer & Hayes, 1991), parental alienation (Blumenkrantz & Tapp, 2001; Brandon, Higgins, Pierce, Tandy & Sileo, 2010), and recently as school connectedness (Hay et al., 2016; McNeely, Nonnemaker & Blum, 2002). Regardless of the term used, all speak to the overlap and relevance of the interconnectedness between the educational system, specifically the school, and a child's caregiver (i.e., parent/family). Because the home and the family are considered the most important contexts for the development of the child (e.g., academics, aspirations, educational outcomes, psychological well-being), the educational system must consider the parent/family to be of significant importance when viewing the child as a learner and social being (Blue-Banning, Summers, Frankland, Nelson & Beegle, 2004; Bronfenbrenner & Morris, 2006). Research supports the benefits of this parent-school connectedness for families, teachers and learners, particularly in outcomes for children/youth with disabilities (Dunlap & Fox, 2007; Turnbull, Turnbull, Erwin, Soodak, & Shogren, 2014; Westergard, 2013).

The relevance of home-school partnership is not a new concept. Bronfenbrenner (1979) theorised that children and their parents/families needed to be at the centre of the learning process and that parents/families, schools and the community should be connected. He argued that parental connectedness and participation were imperative to positive life-long learner outcomes (Bronfenbrenner, 1974, 1979). Vygotsky (1978), in his socio-cultural theory of human development, also discussed the importance of a collaborative partnership among parents, teachers and administrators in the overall learning and education of children/youth.

While most all agree on the importance of parent connectedness to the learning environments of children/youth, recently parents/families have changed tremendously and many suggest that educational institutions have not adapted well to these changes (Edwards, 2016; Hanson & Lynch, 2013; Lynch & Hanson, 2011). Home life today differs more than ever (e.g., significant adults in the home, language spoken, educational level, economic level, culture) (Brown & Brandon, 2009; Knopf & Swick, 2008). Ramirez (2001) found that parents and families feel lost in the educational maze, that their typical resources (e.g., family, community) are not always available and they don't know how to access typical systems (e.g., schools, mental health) for support.

Because families/parents are not a homogeneous group, the evolution of the family unit requires educators to re-evaluate programs that are in place to enhance parent connectedness. School officials and teachers must consider new and inventive methods to develop and maintain relationships with the parents and families with whom they interact (Edwards, 2016). This involves a paradigm-shift from the old top-down model of connectedness (e.g., teachers schedule a meeting and the parents attend) to one of interpersonal relationships that grow over time (e.g., parents given an interaction menu). The changing definitions of parent/family may impact these relationships (Weiss, Caspe & Lopez, 2006).

A working definition of parent/family

All children/youth come from families in which the individual characteristics of the members strengthen or limit the unit (Christenson, 2006). When a child has a disability, the response of the family members may differ according to the characteristics of the disability (e.g., severity, age of onset) as well as the makeup of the family (e.g., size, number of members, number of caregivers). Because of the synergistic nature of the family system and the societal changes that occur, educators must consider a working definition of parent/family, acknowledging that the characterisation of a parent and the composition of a family are social structures that can change over time.

Each school must be responsible for developing a definition of parent/family that meets the demographic composition of the individual site. This definition takes into consideration the individual heterogeneity of the students and the parent/family composition that resides within the school community as well as provides a wealth of information for the development of a parent connectedness program with which to engage families. Research indicates that considering the specific composition of the school, student and parent population increases family engagement (Jordan, Orozco & Averett, 2002; Mapp, 2003). Edwards (2016) referred to this as using the reality of the individual school to define parents and families with whom educators will interact.

TABLE 8.1 Characteristics to consider in the development of a working definition of parent/family

1. Use the term family as much as possible. It is a more encompassing term, as many children/youth do not live with a parent. Many children/youth today live with grandparents, an aunt, an uncle, foster parents or others. This more closely reflects today's reality.
2. The economic situation of the community in which the school is located must be considered. Do not use this as a stereotype of families, but as a tool for understanding a characteristic that may be stressing to the family.
3. Consider the factor of time. Allow the family to define the amount of time available for school activities and involvement.
4. Know all languages and cultures of the families. The school must reflect the community in which it resides as well as welcome differences in language and culture.
5. Make sure that as the definition of parent/family evolves it is based on knowledge of how the family can contribute to the child's education and not on the agendas of teachers or administrators.
6. The strength of the family unit must be represented. New definitions should not be based on a "deficit" model. All families and children have strengths.

While considering the composition of the school and its community involves typical demographic considerations (e.g., languages spoken, economics, diversity of families, disability, educational levels, family composition) in the definition, Kroth and Edge (2007) encouraged teachers and administrators to expand the definition to include six points (see Table 8.1). These allow teachers and administrators to have a precise definition of the parents and families with whom they will develop interpersonal connected relationships. It considers more than numbers or census data points that typically are used to define parents/families in a school and creates a more robust picture of the parent(s) or family as they function within the specific community in which the school is located. This well-rounded picture provides a starting point for the school to begin its development of a site-based parent/family connectedness initiative that considers the composition of the families who will interact with school personnel.

Factors impacting parent connectedness

Being a parent, participating in a family and raising a healthy child are sometimes a daunting responsibility that can impact the connectedness of a parent/family to the school environment. Parents/families generally receive no parenting education, may live in communities with no family or friends, may experience economic hardships, may be learning a new culture or language and may be fearful of the school as a socio-governmental agency (Edwards, 2016; Koonce & Harper, 2005). Because the parent/family is the primary force contributing to the development of children and youth in a positive, neutral or negative manner, hurdles to the school–parent relationship must be identified in order to strengthen the connections (Family Strengthening Policy Center, 2007; Zarrett & Lerner, 2008). Educators and administrators must be aware of the factors that impact school–parent connectedness in order to design programs that support interpersonal relationships with parents, without ignoring the school–parent context as a whole (Christenson, 2003; Comer & Haynes, 1991; Gavin & Greenfield, 1998).

However, parent-family-school connectedness is not a one-way street. That is to say, often the hurdles are internal to the school philosophy or attitudes held by educators and administrators. Although educators indicate they want collaborative partnerships with parents/families, a gap exists between what they put into actual practice and the relationships that are developed (Edwards, 2016; McWilliam, Maxwell & Sloper, 1999; Sanders, 1999). This often is the result of the unequal power and authority in the relationship between parents and school professionals (Blue-Banning, Turnbull & Pereira, 2000). This *power-over* relationship can result in parents/families withdrawing from interacting with educators because the relationship no longer meets their needs or becomes demoralising.

Dunst (2000) found that the gap between evidence-based practices of collaborative partnerships and their implementation often is a failure of the system to understand the construct of *connected partnerships*. That is to say, the system is attempting to implement a program that has not considered the internal as well as external factors that may impede success. Central to the development of a site-based, parent-family-school program focused on connectedness is an understanding of these elements and their impact on the interpersonal relationships, collaboration, trust, and empowerment of the family over time. The literature has identified four integral areas for educators to explore as they begin to develop their parent-family-school connectedness initiative: (a) assumptions that are held by school personnel about the families, parents and students who live in the community in which the school is located, (b) the preservice or inservice training experienced by teachers within the school, (c) the cultural, linguistic, ethnic and economic differences between educators and the population they serve and (d) the stressors and strengths of parents/families rearing children with disabilities (Edwards, 2016; Hanson & Lynch, 2013; Kroth & Edge, 2007). Through the exploration of these areas, school personnel can develop a better understanding of problems that may exist internally or externally that may impede the successful implementation of a program.

Incorrect assumptions

As school demographics change, there often is a mismatch between the life experiences of educators and administrators and the community in which the school is located (Hanson & Lynch, 2013). This can result in potential biases held by school personnel that interfere with forming connected relationships with parents and families (Edwards, 2016). In order to form interpersonal relationships with parents/families and for connectedness to develop, teachers must hone their abilities to know themselves and the impact of their prior experiences on their current assumptions. This involves reflecting upon how their beliefs, attitudes and interactions are similar or different to the parents and families represented in their school;

and ultimately how these facilitate or hinder the formation of connected relationships with parents. This introspective focus provides information concerning an individual's ability to work with those who differ, along with valuable information for creating professional development modules for school personnel.

Through the honest examination of assumptions, both incorrect and correct, school personnel can move beyond the closed, educator-based system of their school to an open system that involves parents/families in a strong and connected community of practice (Wenger, McDermott & Snyder, 2002). This reassessment views parents/families as important members of the learning team and encourages them to assist in the success of their children (Libby, 2004).

Poor training of educators

Unfortunately, personnel preparation programs, both preservice and inservice, have been negligent in teaching and promoting the need for the development and fostering of the interconnectedness among school professionals and parents/families (Greenwood & Hickman, 1991; Winton, 2000). Research indicates that during preservice training only 23% of the participants had family involvement experiences, and 70% said they relied on their own family experiences, not coursework, to understand and develop family relationships when teaching (Mandell & Murray, 2005). This is problematic in that the demographics of the current core of educators, both special and general education, show that most are White, middle class women without disabilities (NCES, 2015).

Often, at the school level, the topic is not addressed in professional development due to the ambivalence felt by educators and administrators concerning parental involvement (Comer & Haynes, 1991; Kroth & Edge, 2007) and that the term means something different to professionals with diverse educational foci (Ascher, 1988). However, educators who experience multiple opportunities to learn how to interact with families and develop family-centred dispositions generalise their learning to their classroom when working with parents and families (Murray & Mandell, 2004). Currently, there appears to be little opportunity for educators to learn in their preservice or inservice training the needed attitudes and skills for family-centred practice (Mulholland & Blecker, 2008).

In order for parents to connect with school personnel, they must feel that the teachers understand them (and their child) and that the school provides them with social comfort (Comer & Haynes, 1991). To do this, educators must have the skills to: (a) form consensus, (b) be sensitive to those who differ from them (e.g., disability, economically, educationally, culturally), (c) be accountable to parents in a realistic manner, (d) develop trust among partners and (e) understand multiple perspectives on issues. At the school level, this involves the provision of professional development for teachers and other service providers to be able to match the specific developmental needs of the children/youth, the attitudes and practices of parents and the school expectations in order to develop a comprehensive program to foster parent-family-school connectedness. This training is particularly important for novice educators who may need support to incorporate new information and for long-time educators who are learning to work with parents who differ from them or who have children with disabilities (Kroth & Edge, 2007).

Cultural, linguistic, ethnic and economic differences

Forging connectedness among parent-family-school involves educators having a deep understanding of the lives, histories and cultures of the families who reside within the school community, particularly when they differ from those of school personnel. Berliner (1986) pointed out that educators have no choice but to learn about each child's unique culture and history when creating learning pathways. The observation also is true when considering the cultural, linguistic, ethnic or economic diversity of the family unit (Araujo, 2009; Ayers, 2016). This involves breaking down the stereotypes that educators may hold about parents/families and the fears parents/families may hold about the school and moving towards a connected goal of working together for better outcomes for all children/youth (Knopf & Swick, 2008; Ramirez, 2001). All participants must recognise the multiple spheres of influence that jigsaw as schools and parents/families work together (Epstein et al., 2009).

When considering culture, language, ethnicity or economics as factors impacting parent-family-school connectedness, two realities exist concerning parent involvement. The first is that not all parents need to be encouraged to become connected to the school, regardless of the family characteristics. These parents are heavily involved in their child's education and need few, if any, incentives to become more involved. Secondly, the literature suggests that this connectedness results from the beliefs of parents/families that the school should give priority to the needs of their child (e.g., disability, social, learning), often to the exclusion of other children and families (Lareau, 2003).

This involves educators considering the previous experiences of the parents with whom they interact in forming interpersonal relationships. The consideration should not be based on pre-conceived notions, but the collection of information from the parents concerning previous experiences with educational systems, comfort level with coming to school and parental beliefs about their role in their child's education (Chrispeels & Rivero, 2001; Drummond & Stipek, 2004; Sheldon, 2002). These data will provide a wealth of knowledge as educators and administrators begin to develop their parent-family-school connectedness initiative in terms of the impact previous experiences or beliefs have on parent-family-school interactions and how to incorporate the findings into the planning of a well-designed program. The collection of the information also will convey respect to the parents/families who live in the community as the school works to understand the specific indicators that may work to hinder a strong connection with those who live within the school boundaries. It will provide an understanding of the socio-cultural diversity of the voices of the parents/families within the full context of their experiences.

Parents/families rearing children with disabilities

Parents/families of children with disabilities have different experiences than most and these must be considered because of the impact the disability has on the family unit (Parke, 2004). Often, the type of disability, severity of the disability and family composition will impact the connectedness of the parent/family with the school (Turnbull et al., 2014). Because these families often have challenges that are not faced by other families, educators and school personnel must take steps to ascertain the different roles members of the family play in the life of their child. Examples include: (a) teaching appropriate cultural norms and rules, (b) providing guidance in social situations, (c) managing their child's medical needs, (d) finding tutoring for their child's academic needs and (e) supervising their child's life outside of the family unit (Heward, 2012; Parke, 2004). All are multidimensional tasks and may directly or indirectly impact the whole family or specific members of the family individually. Hobbs (1978) reminded school personnel that parents/families are the true special educators, in that they are the experts on their child, and that those who work with a student with a disability must view their role as one of being a consultant to the parent.

Considerations that educators must have when working with parents of children with disabilities are child and family specific. Research indicates that the impact of the child/youth on the family (e.g., marriage, parents, siblings) varies (Turnbull et al., 2014). While early research indicated a high divorce rate among two-parent families, this is no longer the case (Urbano & Hodapp, 2007). Parents report that they adapt to their child's condition and that the family unit grows over time (Blacher & Baker, 2007; Dowling, 2007). However, parents often report high stress levels (Lopez, Clifford, Minnes & Ouelletter-Kuntz, 2008), fear for their child's future (Dowling, 2007), being emotionally drained (Kenny & McGilloway, 2007), experiencing a lower quality of life (Bertelli, Bianco, Rossi, Scuticchio & Brown, 2011), and less power in their relationships with the educators who work with their child (Hodge & Runswick-Cole, 2008).

Connected partnerships with parents/families raising a child with a disability ultimately must support the student in attaining equal opportunity in life endeavours, living independently, participating in school offerings and achieving economic self-sufficiency. The development of these relationships relies on the ability of school personnel to acknowledge the unique circumstances of the parent/family and connecting the expertise of the parent/family with the resources of the school (Turnbull et al., 2014). All must work to develop trust, foster respect and share in the decision making to form mutually connected relationships (Blue-Banning et al., 2004).

A well-designed school connectedness program benefits all of the children/youth in a school. The basis of the program must be a review by school personnel of their own assumptions about the community in which their school resides, the knowledge they possess about the members of the community, the biases they may hold about parents/families in the community and about their ability to work with parents who have a child with a disability. Introspection is a personal reality check and allows the educator or administrator to think of parent participation as more than assigning tasks for parents to complete, but a relationship that grows and develops as more interaction occurs. This allows for more non-traditional ways for parents to be involved, family-centred services to be created, parent education services to be provided and teacher professional development to be created. Parents want to be involved; it is up to school personnel to address the factors that may impede parent connectedness.

A new paradigm to foster parent connectedness

Parent involvement initiatives must be a part of a contextually focused school improvement process designed to create positive relationships to support comprehensive child development (Comer & Haynes, 1991). A one-size-fits-all approach will not reflect the fabric of the school or the community in which the school resides. This all-inclusive program must be wide ranging in nature and site based. In short, individual schools must work to develop a parent/family connectedness program that reflects the needs of the students and parents within the community. This is a multidimensional process that involves the commitment of all involved and the understanding that connectedness based on trust and respect grows over time. While the base of the program is school personnel, parents/families must be consulted to the greatest extent possible as the program is constructed. Research finds that when parents are involved, the relationships established enhance their desire to be involved more, and a synergistic relationship of connectedness begins in terms of their participation in their child's educational development (Mapp, 2003).

Collect demographic data

Comprehensive planning always begins with good data. Thus, all planning should begin with the creation of a demographic profile. The first round of data will come from the school district in which the school is located, but these data are not enough. Think of these data as a view from a spaceship out in space of the individual school. These data provide numbers from which to drill down into the specific profile of the school.

School

The true picture of the school, its parents/families and children come from a composite description of the school. This level of information provides a closer view of the school in terms of the community as a whole and the individual families who live in the community. This involves taking the school district data provided and drilling down into the specific neighbourhood served (e.g., families living in apartments, lack of grocery stores, parks, recreation venues, public transportation). The next collection of data involves focusing on the families within the school (e.g., where do they work, diverse groups represented, languages spoken, number of families with children with disabilities, generations of families in the neighbourhood). The more focused the picture, the better understanding school personnel will have of the community in which the family functions and the supports or lack of supports within the community.

Individual classrooms

Once a composite picture is drawn of the school, it is the individual teacher's responsibility to create a classroom profile. This will change yearly and provides rich information of the students and their families. Data to be collected include: (a) size of the family (e.g., adults in the home, siblings, other children in the home), (b) the countries represented by the English learners (EL) in the class, (c) the types of disabilities represented in the classroom and services provided in the past, (d) types of school interactions that parents/families feel comfortable with and those that intimidate them, (e) language spoken at home, (f) employment of adults (caregivers) in the home, (g) interests and hobbies that the family engages in as a unit and (h) any other information the parent/family feels comfortable providing. This information provides the educator with family-centred data by which to begin understanding each child's family, and helps develop a baseline from which to create a trusting and respectful relationship with the family (Ayers, 2016).

Solicit parental information

The final data to be collected comes from the parent/family. Because partnerships built among families and professionals benefit all children/youth (particularly those with disabilities), it is important to collect information from the family unit concerning their previous experiences with professional partnerships (Turnbull et al., 2014). These relationships encompass the expertise and resources of the parent/ family as well as the professionals involved with the child/youth (Turnbull et al., 2014). Collecting this information provides individual teachers with information concerning the past history of the family in terms of collaborative relationships, services provided and the family's satisfaction with those school partnerships.

A valid and reliable instrument for collecting this information is the *Beach Center Family-Professional Partnership Scale* (Summers et al., 2005). The scale is comprised of 18 items that ask the parents/caregivers to provide their perceptions concerning satisfaction with their relationships with the professionals (e.g., teachers) who work with their children. While the scale was developed primarily for use with families in which there is a child with a disability, it can be used with all parents as it focuses on two domains relevant to professional relationships in general (child-focused relationships and family-focused relationships). The survey items cover a range of foci, from "my child's teacher helps me gain skills or information to understand my child's needs" to "my child's teacher is friendly." Each item is rated on a 5-point Likert scale, ranging from 1 (very dissatisfied) to 5 (very satisfied). This information is critical for each teacher to understand previous relationships the parent/family has experienced and to identify areas on which to focus as they work to build a connected relationship with the family.

A second valid instrument that may be used is the *Barriers to School Involvement Survey* (Reglin, King, Losike-Sedimo & Ketterer, 2003). The survey asks parents to respond to 30 items that range from "the school does not let me know about the good things my child does" to "the teachers use language I do not understand." The questions are rated using a 4-point Likert scale ranging from 1 (not a problem) to 4 (always a problem). This instrument focuses on elements of the school or relationship process that results in parents feeling alienated from the school. The results can help identify critical points at which parents begin to lose their connectedness to the school as a system and to teachers in particular.

Once all data and information are collected and analysed, a well-rounded picture emerges of the strengths and needs of the parents/families in relation to the school. The literature indicates that all parents need some things, but not all parents need all things (Kroth & Edge, 2007). These data also reflect a realistic picture of the family context and allows teachers and administrators to begin to assess their school in terms of its needs and strengths when working with parents and families.

Assess the reality of the school in terms of data collected

The demographic and survey data collected from the school district, the school, the classrooms and the parents must be aggregated into a complete picture of the reality of the school. This picture should be revisited yearly as data change over time and parent information provided on the surveys will change and grow as the school institutes its connectedness program.

The reality of the school at a specific point in time should be assessed using *ecological theory*; that is based on the data collected in terms of the interdependent and multiple systems that interact and impact the child's development and the relationships with parents/families. The assessment should include: (a) the *microsystems* involved in the school (e.g., home, classrooms), (b) the *mesosystems* or how the microsystems interrelate, (c) the *exosystems* that influence the microsystems (e.g., the work environment of the parent that supports or hinders parental involvement, transportation issues that hinder parental involvement), and (d) *macrosystems* that exist in the social and cultural environment in which the school resides as well as local and national educational policies that may impact the functioning of the school (Sheridan & Kratochwill, 2007).

Questions to be asked of the data at this point in time should be (a) what picture emerges of the families (e.g., income level, educational level, languages spoken), (b) what picture emerges of the parent-professional partnerships currently in place at the school as reported by the parents (e.g., teacher honesty, teacher availability, teacher skills as viewed by the parent(s), respect, trust), and (c) what barriers there are to school involvement as reported by the parents (e.g., communication between school and home, school not valuing the opinion of the parent, lack of caring of teachers and administrators). From the questions and a review of the data collected, a robust picture of the school emerges identifying the strengths and needs of the school in terms of parent connectedness. It is important to remember the data provide a realistic point to begin to define parental connectedness and create a program to enhance it within the school building.

Define parent connectedness in relation to the school site

Positive home-school connectedness is a multidimensional construct that grows over time and across educational settings (Ou, 2005). This involves linkages across school levels (e.g., elementary, middle, high school), transition points (e.g., pre-school to formal schooling) and relationships among all involved. It includes programs that support and help the family sustain its connectedness to the system as their child moves through school. This becomes extremely important for families with children who have disabilities, as caregivers often report being alienated from their child's school (Kroth & Edge, 2007; Turnbull, Turnbull, Erwin, Soodak & Shogren, 2014).

As educators begin to define parent-family-school connectedness, the definition must be broader than the usual parent involvement (e.g., reading to their child, attending parent conferences). Parent-family-school connectedness has its roots in the relationship between the home (e.g., parents, families) and the school (e.g., teachers, administrators) (McWilliam, Tocci & Harbin, 1998). This involves the formal and informal connections between the family and the various individuals in the educational setting (e.g., teachers, service providers). While parent involvement is a component, connectedness is a more personal relationship between school personnel and the family/parent and should be viewed through an interpersonal lens rather than one that is task based. Connectedness takes a broader view of parent-family-school relationships and considers all of the contexts that impact parenting within a specific community setting (Weiss, Caspe & Lopez, 2006).

Thus, a definition of parent-family-school connectedness must be individually crafted for each school and be based on the demographic data collected as well as the survey data provided by the parents. If school personnel recognise the knowledge of the parent/family unit, then the definition of connectedness that emerges is based on the personal contexts of the individual parents-families and the school in which their children are educated. This definition is imperative in fostering good communication that results in strong interpersonal relationships to maximise student success in school and in life beyond the boundaries of school.

Because the definition of parent-family-school connectedness is site-based, the literature provides a roadmap to consider in the crafting of the definition (Hay & Winn, 1989; Koonce & Harper, 2005; Kroth & Edge, 2007; Park & Turnbull, 2003) (see Table 8.2). The significance of the definition in laying the groundwork for a parent-family-school connectedness program cannot be underestimated. When working with parents/families with children with disabilities this becomes

TABLE 8.2 Considerations in crafting a parent-family-school connectedness definition

1. Consider the specific family contexts represented in the community in which the school is located.
2. Put interpersonal relationships and collaboration at the centre of the definition.
3. Make sure the definition adopts an open understanding of what constitutes a family.
4. Think out of the box and consider non-traditional components of connectedness.
5. Make the definition family centred and focused on the family and child, not the school.
6. The definition should be meaningful, not artificial, and consider the immediate community served by the school.
7. Recognition should be given to the fact that parents/families differ greatly in their willingness, ability, and availability to interact. Definitions should not be task specific.
8. Solicit parents-families concerning their perceptions on the construct of connectedness. This will ensure a shared vision.

very important, as the goal is to form a connected partnership that will lead to communication and the ability to resolve disputes as a family-centred team (Osher & Osher, 2002).

Create a parental connectedness initiative

Based on the demographic data collected, the parental responses to the surveys and the school-based definition of connectedness, a parental initiative can be created. This plan of action must acknowledge the intersecting relationships (e.g., teachers, parents, administrators, service providers) needed to create a unified set of expectations and a sense of shared purpose of all partners (Ayers, 2016; Edwards, 2016). Connectedness does not occur in a vacuum; it must be planned, honest and acknowledge the expertise of the parents. The research indicates that the most successful programs in engendering parent-school connectedness are those that offer a variety of ways for families/parents to participate in their child's school environment (Comer & Haynes, 1991; Cotton & Wikelund, 1989; Epstein et al., 2009; Kroth & Edge, 2007). These programs recognise that parents do want to participate (Kroth & Edge, 2007), but differ in their willingness, ability, time, training and knowledge for involvement (Edwards, 2016). Often parents/families simply need accommodations to facilitate their connectedness. The most successful parent involvement programs are those that provide a variety of roles and activities from which parents can select based on their work schedules, preferences, comfort level and their capabilities (Comer & Haynes, 1991; Cotton & Wikelund, 1989). Kroth and Edge (2007) found that parents wanted more non-traditional ways to be connected to their child's education and that these should be oriented to the child's needs and not the more traditional involvement (e.g., volunteering at school, attending assemblies). Over time, the goal is that the school views the parents as more than volunteers or fundraisers and sees them as connected partners of the school's learning community (Comer & Haynes, 1991; Edwards, 2016).

A tiered system

Connectedness cannot be mandated from the top down or through governmental policies. It must be organic and grow over time. The relationships involved in connectedness are based on trust, respect and flexibility. It views those involved in the child's learning environment and home as experts, all bringing unique knowledge and talents to the shared goal of educating the child/youth. This unique group of individuals shares a concern (i.e., the child/youth), discusses problems, celebrates successes, comes to consensus and interacts on an ongoing basis.

As the school begins to develop its connectedness initiative, it must take into consideration the data collected and the definition created to develop a program that recognises the uniqueness of the parents/families in the school (Kroth & Edge, 2007). This allows those involved to move beyond the boundaries of the school system and understand the relationships between the child and parent, school and parent, child and school, child and teacher and teacher and parent. In this manner, the heterogeneity of the participants is recognised, making the focus of connectedness less narrow. Viewing all through the lens of their totality (e.g., culture, disability, relationships) provides a better understanding of the ability of the individuals to form connected relationships and what must be in place to facilitate their development.

A tiered program provides parents with a framework from which to select when considering school involvement (Comer & Haynes, 1991; Epstein et al., 2009; Kroth & Edge, 2007). This involves parents selecting the level at which they currently feel most comfortable in participating and to which they believe they can commit. All levels must carry responsibility and all must involve some interactions with teachers and school staff (Comer & Haynes, 1991). The tiered approach should be reviewed annually as connected relationships form and grow over time.

Comer and Haynes (1991) suggested three tiers of parental involvement, based on the school make up and composition.

1. Level Three, defined as general participation (e.g., parent conferences).
2. Level Two, defined as a more involved participation (e.g., helping in the classroom, volunteering to support school programs).
3. Level One, defined as joining the school team (e.g., being elected to a position on the school PTA, participating on the School Planning and Management Team).

In a five-part framework, Epstein (1988) included the school as a function of the obligations of parents.

1. Type One is the basic obligation of the parent (e.g., communicating with the teacher).
2. Type Two is the basic obligation of the school (e.g., developing a connectedness program).
3. Type Three is more parental involvement at the school (e.g., attending conferences, working in the classroom).

4. Type Four focuses on parents involved in learning at home (e.g., reading with their child, helping with homework).
5. Type Five involves the parent in school governance and advocacy.

The Harvard Family Research Project (Caspe, Lopez & Wolos, 2007; Kreider, Caspe, Kennedy & Weiss, 2007; Weiss, Caspe & Lopez, 2006) presents a three-tiered connectedness framework and ties the components to child/youth outcomes at the early childhood level, the elementary school level and the middle/high school level. The three tiers for parents with young children involve (a) parenting (e.g., building the parent–child relationship, participation in child-centred activities), (b) home-school relationships (e.g., communication on a regular basis with school, participation in at-school activities as defined by the school) and (c) responsibility for learning outcomes (e.g., reading in the home, parent–child conversations). For parents with primary school age children, the three tiers are the same, but the options differ (a) parenting (e.g., building the parent–child relationship, developing linkages with the community), (b) home-school relationships (e.g., communication on a regular basis with the school, participation in school events, participation in formal parent involvement programs) and (c) responsibility for learning outcomes (e.g., supporting literacy, helping with homework, managing their child's education, having high expectations of their child). At the middle and high school levels, there is recognition that the relationship among family members changes with the developing independence of the child/youth. The three tiers at this age include (a) parenting (e.g., changing in style, relationship changes), (b) home-school relationship (e.g., communication changes, participation in school-based organisations, participation in college outreach programs, participation in transition programs) and (c) responsibility for learning outcomes (e.g., homework management, educational expectations, encouragement for post-secondary education, encouragement for living independently).

When viewing the three examples, it is not the specifics that are important, but that a framework can be developed. The strength of a tiered framework is that it is created corresponding to the demographics of the school, the definition of connectedness created by educators and administrators, and the strengths and needs of the parents. The goal of a tiered framework of connectedness is that as trust grows and relationships develop, parents will move among the tiers and become more comfortable assuming a greater and greater role in their child's educational environment.

A parent connectedness initiative involves the parent involvement tasks outlined in a tiered system, but it is not defined by this involvement. Connectedness has its roots in the relationship, involving trust and respect, between the parent/family and the various individuals in the school. When the construct of connectedness is present, parental involvement is the natural outcome (Hay et al., 2016). Through a systematic and structured review of the school setting, educators and administrators are better able to understand the contextual connections among all partners, including parents. Through this reality-based plan of action, parental connectedness can be achieved and grown over time.

Conclusion

In the second decade of the 21st century, it is imperative to maximise the educational outcomes of children/youth, particularly those with disabilities. This must involve stronger connections among the school, parents/families, teachers, and communities. When the home and school are connected and the school and parents are actively engaged in the development of strong connections, there is a greater likelihood of long-term positive educational, social and psychological outcomes for children/youth (Wilkinson-Lee, Zhang, Nuno & Wilhelm, 2011). While the home is considered the primary socialisation context, schools (e.g., teachers, service providers) are becoming more and more influential for the academic and social development of students who reside within their care (Stewart, 2008). Thus, the development of parent-family-school connectedness initiatives is simply the ethical thing to do. In the end, these will create synergistic relationships in which connectedness is the norm and successful student educational and lifelong outcomes are the result.

THEORY TO PRACTICE

Suggestions can be divided into four areas:
Policymakers can…

- Develop policies that provide supports (e.g., money, time) for individual schools to develop their capacities to design effective parent connectedness programs. This should involve dynamic internal programs and interactive outreach programs that are responsive to the needs of parents
- Create regular opportunities for parents to be involved in policy making (e.g., invitations to meetings, holding meetings in the local community, reports in multiple languages)
- Support initiatives to integrate parent-family-school connectedness across school levels (e.g., early childhood, elementary, secondary)
- Invest in evaluations of family connectedness strategies to provide data to decision-making bodies concerning the effectiveness of program impact on academic learning, behaviour, motivation, and graduation rates
- Provide incentives for the community to get involved in their neighbourhood school
- Develop policies to help parents easily obtain the information they need to support their child's success in school

Teacher educators can…

- Create collaborative programs that involve preservice special and general education students to learn the skills of communication to work with *all* parents

- Involve general and special education students in collaborative programs in which they learn the interpersonal skills needed to work with parents who may be in crisis (e.g., families of children with disabilities, families living in poverty)
- Develop professional development programs that focus on a tiered system of learning to teach working with parents and families (e.g., Tier 1 = 1st field experience, Tier 2 = 2nd field experience, Tier 3 = student teaching).
- Connect research about working with parents to the interventions and strategies taught in coursework
- Build a culturally responsive knowledge base for teacher educators that includes all facets of diversity, including disability
- Involve students in their preservice training in reflective activities concerning predetermined attitudes and biases that may impact their work with students and families who differ from them

School leaders can...

- Create a non-traditional connectedness program that considers the parent/ family and their ability to be involved
- Create a parent/teacher management team that sets a welcoming tone for parents and members of the community to interact with the school
- Be committed to a strong parent-family-school connectedness program
- Involve community agencies, feeder schools, public and private service providers in the school connectedness program to address family–parent–school issues
- Empower teachers to learn about the parents/families of the children in their classrooms on a yearly basis
- Empower parents to participate in the school through trust building, respectful collaboration systems, and sustainable connectedness programs
- Systematise continuous parent-family-school connectedness programs so that there is a seamless transition from school level to school level. School connectedness exists across a continuum

Teachers can...

- Become involved in community projects, even if they do not live within the school community. To be seen in a community, is to be considered part of it
- Spend time learning about the students in your classroom. Read and explore about diversity issues, disability issues and parental issues about which you have little knowledge
- Develop a classroom communication system with parental input
- Seek out training to develop a strong confidence level of working with parents/families who differ. This should involve strategies for working with

children who have disabilities, working with students learning English, and learning about other cultures
- Work to learn about parents/families goals for their child, their perspectives on learning and behaviour, and their comfort level with the formal education process
- Be consistent in showing respect to build trusting relationships over time. Be aware that the past experiences of many families with the school system may have been negative – some may not even feel comfortable entering the school building as a result

9

STRATEGIES TO PROMOTE SCHOOL CONNECTEDNESS

Today's students have more complex needs than students of the past, and the old school paradigms do not address these needs (McLaughlin & Gray, 2015). Between 40–60% of students are disengaged from school by high school (Blum, 2005b), and in large urban schools only 50% of students graduate (National Research Council and the Institute of Medicine, 2004). Despite the lack of agreement over the terminology and definition of school connectedness, there is agreement in the literature from the various fields of psychology, sociology, health and education that school reform is necessary in order to best address the developmental needs of all students at all levels to increase their sense of connectedness to their schools. Some regard this as a soft approach, due to the increasing focus on accountability and standards, but in reality, school connectedness has a significant impact on student achievement (Blum, 2005b).

Past research has focused on how schools, their climate and organisation/structure affect students' academic achievement, but current research strives to discover how schools affect students' well-being and future success. School connectedness is a key protective factor for students. This equates to better post-school outcomes and less risky behaviour such as violence, anti-social and sexual behaviour, drug use and dropping out (Blum, 2005b).

This is particularly pertinent when viewing the school experience of students with disabilities, as their numbers, especially that of students with emotional and behavioural disabilities (EBD), have increased over the last two decades (McLaughlin & Gray, 2015). Students with disabilities typically experience difficulties with academic achievement, and the socio-emotional and behavioural aspects of schooling (Kauffman & Landrum, 2013; Kern, 2015; Lane et al., 2006), which may negatively impact their feeling of connectedness to their schools. They may have an impaired ability to create and maintain relationships with their teachers and peers, one of the pillars of connectedness. This population is at an increased risk for developing depression and anxiety and health risk behaviours such as drug and alcohol misuse, weapons possession, smoking and sexual intercourse. One of the goals of school connectedness is that all students feel connected and a part of the school community. Edwards (2015) suggests that this is not just about students with disabilities being included in general education classrooms, but about students accessing and contributing to the things that school and mainstream society has to offer. In order to accomplish this, early intervention is crucial; students must be identified as soon as they are seen as being vulnerable.

Research has shown a strong relationship between school connectedness and school attendance, finishing school, higher grades, higher test scores, avoidance of health risk behaviours (DASH-CDC, 2009). Students feel supported by adults at school when they see them dedicating time, interest, effort and support to them. They want to feel that adults care for them as people in addition to being concerned with their academic achievement. Students want teachers who are respectful and fair, willing to listen to them, make them feel like they are competent, encourage self-determination, are advocates for students and are positive (McLaughlin & Gray, 2015).

Thomas (2015) postulates that traditionally designed school systems separate more then they connect, disconnecting students from the real world and separating them from each other based on a caste system of accomplishments, abilities or backgrounds. She recommends that schools be redesigned. She believes that design principles can guide schools to innovate together, rather than in a patchy isolated way, especially when design principles with a learning mindset that incorporate the values and beliefs of the school are used. The goal is to create a school culture that values enquiry and experimentation.

So how does a school accomplish what seems like such a daunting task? The focus of this chapter is on research-based strategies to promote school connectedness for students with disabilities. Although there is limited research that focuses specifically on students with disabilities, prevalence rates suggest that this population was represented in studies of the effects of school connectedness. This chapter outlines ways in which schools can implement these strategies school-wide and in the classroom. School leadership teams are key players in this endeavour, along with teachers, students, parents and the community. Several models and programs that underpin whole-school approaches to connectedness through school organisational development, health promotion and an emphasis on partnerships between staff, students and parents are presented, along with suggestions for further research.

Evidence based practices

Christenson, Reschly, Appleton, Berman-Young, Spanjers and Varro (2008) highlight that interventions to increase school connectedness must not be just about academics and attendance, they must also take into account students' social and emotional needs, as focusing on academics only serves to ignore the fact that the classroom is social and emotional, especially with adolescents. They stress the need for an assessment-to-intervention link to design data-based interventions, both universal (school-wide) and targeted (individualised). Effective practices have a positive effect on students' motivation because they address competence, control, beliefs about school and the value of education and a sense of belonging. Schools need to recognise that engagement is not a static student attribute, but a changeable state, strongly influenced by the environment at school, home and with peers.

The *Wingspread Declaration on School Connections* is a synthesis of core principles of school connectedness designed to guide U.S. schools (Blum, 2005a). The Declaration was based on a detailed review of research on school engagement and connectedness, to support school systems' use of what research has found creates schools that students feel connected to. Blum's research demonstrated that there are three school characteristics that help young people feel connected to school: high academic standards with strong teacher support, student and adult relationships that are positive and respectful, and schools that are physically and emotionally safe. There is strong scientific evidence that suggests when these three factors are present, there is an increase in academic achievement, school completion rates, motivation, classroom engagement and school attendance, and a decrease in bullying, fighting, vandalism and absenteeism. These findings apply across racial, ethnic and income groups. There is also strong evidence that a student who feels connected to school is less likely to exhibit disruptive behaviour, school violence, substance and tobacco use, emotional distress, early age of first sexual experience, transport risk taking behaviour and violence risk taking (Blum, 2005b; Chapman, Buckley, Sheehan, Shochet, & Romaniuk, 2011).

The *Wingspread Declaration on School Connections* suggested that the most effective strategies for increasing the school connectedness include:

- having high standards and expectations and providing academic support to all students so that they can meet those standards
- collectively creating fair and consistent disciplinary policies and fairly enforcing them
- fostering trusting relationships among students, teachers, staff, school leadership teams and families
- ensuring that teachers are capable and skilled in content, teaching techniques and classroom management to meet the needs of diverse learners
- supporting high family expectations for school performance and school completion, and
- ensuring that every student feels close to at least one supportive adult at school.

Not many studies have evaluated the impact of singular interventions designed to foster school connectedness (DASH-CDC, 2009). Many have implemented more than one strategy at a time, making it difficult to isolate the results of a single intervention. Because of this, most of the strategies suggested in the literature are recommended as best practice rather than evidence based practices. The DASH-CDC (2009) has proposed that four main factors improve a student's sense of connectedness to school: (a) adult support, (b) belonging to a positive peer group, (c) commitment to education and (d) school environment. This is an expansion of the earlier results of the *Wingspread Declaration,* and in line with the domains proposed in Chapter 2 and represented in Figure 2.1: (a) school bonding, (b) school attachment, (c) school engagement and (d) school climate.

The DASH-CDC suggested six strategies to increase school connectedness. These strategies are based on research literature in the fields of health, psychology, sociology and education. A description of each strategy, along with recommendations on how they can be implemented, appears below. There has been little change in the suggested strategies since the CDC published them in 2009; they have been widely accepted internationally. However, there have been some recent suggestions of research-based practices to support the implementation of the six strategies. Those that were added after 2009 are integrated throughout, under the appropriate strategy, with a citation to provide evidence of its efficacy.

Strategies suggested for improving school connectedness

The first strategy is *designing decision-making processes that include the voices of staff, students, families, and the community*, leading to empowerment for all involved and increased academic achievement. In order to implement this strategy, school leaders should collaborate with teachers, staff, students and families to develop a shared vision of high standards for learning and behaviour. This collaboration should be expanded to encourage teacher and staff input in efforts to improve school climate and student connectedness. Teams of students, parents and school staff can be formed to develop school policies and plan school activities. These teams can also assist in writing grant proposals and seeking support from community businesses. Teams can work with school leadership teams to make decisions about how school resources are used (people, time, facilities, funds). Another important team function is to work together to make changes to the school's physical environment to make it more pleasant. This would involve relatively small changes, such as removing graffiti and cleaning the school.

Assigning students developmentally appropriate levels of responsibility in classroom decision-making and management can foster students' involvement. Student voices can also be heard through feedback mechanisms to give feedback to their teachers and empower them to lead parent teacher conferences where they are actively involved in the discussions. Collaboration should also include community partners. Encourage community partners to provide services for students and families at the school (health, dental, child care, substance abuse treatment). This will make students and families feel more like a part of the school community, and give them a sense of ownership in the school.

The second strategy is to *support families in the active involvement in their children's academic and school life*. The school can accomplish this by providing parent training programs that give parents opportunities to increase their skills in areas that will allow them to be more involved in their children's school life (English courses, high school equivalency diplomas, communication, parenting and leadership skills). Other workshops can support parents in acquiring academic support, parenting and behaviour management skills. This will give parents the opportunity to meet and get to know one another, as well as working together with school staff. Training workshops should be provided via alternate formats (online, teleconference, correspondence) in order to reach parents who live far away, have difficulty with mobility or have family situations or work schedules that make it difficult for them to attend in person.

Parents can be encouraged to support learning at home. They can assist with homework, provide a space and supplies for their children to study and help their children with time management. In order to coordinate family involvement with their children's education, staff members can be liaisons to specific students and their families to support them in discovering ways that they can be more involved in the school. They can make sure that both the student and family feel welcome at school and connect them with community resources. To enable parents to participate, provide opportunities for involvement that fits with parents' diverse schedules, abilities and skills, and provide childcare, transportation and virtual or alternative meeting locations. To ensure that all parents can be involved, provide online and paper-based information in the languages most commonly spoken at home, and provide interpreters to assist during meetings and events. Regular meetings with parents to discuss student behaviour, grades and accomplishments will go a long way to getting and keeping parents involved. During times of transition, such as from primary to secondary school, it may be beneficial to conduct these meetings in students' homes.

The third strategy is to *provide students with the academic, emotional, and social skills necessary to be successfully engaged in school.* To engage a diverse range of students, consider providing one-on-one tutoring, opportunities for students to be involved in positive academic competition within and among schools (debates, science fair projects), and opportunities for extended learning opportunities during summer and term breaks to support students with their academic and social skills. Support students in developing non-academic skills such as problem solving, communication, conflict resolution, self-control, negotiation, anger management, sharing and good manners. This skills training should be incorporated into the K–12 curriculum, with classroom lessons that explore empathy, fairness, kindness and social responsibility, and explicit teaching of refusal and resistance skills. Reinforce these skills by engaging students in service learning activities such as school/classroom chores, peer tutoring, office and teacher assistance. Students should be provided with opportunities during the school day for students to identify and express their feelings. School sporting events and physical education classes can be used to promote the concepts of teamwork, sportsmanship, fair play and nonviolence.

The fourth strategy suggested is to *use effective classroom management and pedagogy to create a positive learning environment.* This should entail the use of Positive Behavioural Support (PBS) strategies (Osher, Bear, Sprague & Doyle, 2010), beginning with the design and communication of clear expectations for academics and behaviour that are developmentally appropriate and consistent across students. The classroom environment should be organised in a way that promotes positive behaviour and prevents discipline problems from occurring in the first place. Give students opportunity to have leadership positions in the classroom and allow their voices and opinions to be heard.

Strategies such as increasing instructional quality and how instruction is delivered and providing supplemental support can enhance student engagement in the classroom (Christenson et al., 2008). Tailor teaching methods and classroom management strategies to the diverse needs of the students. Lessons should be linked to standards and sequentially built upon prior lessons, with the goals of the lesson clearly communicated to students and related to their lives and the world. The curriculum should be relevant, be matched to student abilities and incorporate student choice in activities (Christenson et al., 2008). Use a variety of teaching strategies and group work to foster problem solving, critical thinking and skills for working with others. These can include interactive and experiential activities such as group discussions, peer assisted instruction, role-plays and problem solving (Christenson et al., 2008). Encourage open, respectful communication, and if viewpoints differ, allow students to challenge and debate to teach them respect for diverse opinions and perspectives. It is highly recommended that teachers use continuous assessment to make data-based decisions about behaviour management and teaching and learning. Although the DASH-CDC (2009) also recommends reducing class size, this may be a logistical impossibility in some schools, and Blum (2005b) asserts that classroom culture is significantly more important than class size. Schools should develop a reward system for academic and extracurricular achievements, but at the same time, encourage intrinsic reinforcement by displaying student work and accomplishments.

Strategy number five is *professional development for all school staff, in order for all stakeholders to have the skills to facilitate meeting the diverse needs of students.* First and foremost, teachers should be provided with professional development that supports them in creating an engaging learning environment in their classrooms, one that emphasises positive behaviours and values. Home school collaboration will be enhanced if teachers learn strategies to communicate effectively with parents and involve them in school. Schools should also provide teachers with professional development on all curricula the school is learning and effective methods to teach it. This professional development will be meaningless, however, if the school leaders do not take steps to ensure that teachers have the materials, time, resources and support to teach the curriculum in the manner they are trained to. This learning and support can be enhanced by the promotion of staff peer learning through the formation of learning teams, where inexperienced teachers can observe master teachers using effective pedagogy and management techniques. Along these lines, schools should develop a mentoring program for new teachers, so teachers that can share their knowledge and expertise can support them.

The last strategy is to *foster trusting and caring relationships that foster open communication among all stakeholders.* This strategy is crucial to improving students' sense of connectedness to their schools, as peer and teacher relationships have been repeatedly found to have a significant impact on school connectedness (Christenson et al., 2008). The program *Check and Connect* has a strong research base and was created to promote engagement through relationship building, problem solving, and persistence. A mentor works with students and families for at least two years, daily monitoring student behaviour and educational progress, and intervening when necessary (Christenson et al., 2008).

Changes to the organisational structure of the school can facilitate communication and relationship building. For example, organising the structure so that teachers stay with the same students for consecutive years provides continuity in learning and stronger teacher–student relationships. Making the school building available outside of school hours for recreation and/or health promotion programs has been shown to increase student and parent feelings of being part of the school community. School-wide activities that allow students to learn about and celebrate diversity encourage students to form connections with one another and increase their respect for diversity. School-wide activities also help to lessen hierarchical divisions between older and younger students and students of all abilities by providing opportunities for interaction. University outreach programs increase academic achievement and exposure to local campuses (Christenson et al., 2008).

To strengthen relationships between students and school staff, provide opportunities for students to work with adults in helping roles, and encourage their involvement on school committees. Adult school staff can provide an example for students by modelling respectful behaviour towards students and each other. Staff should greet each student by name and make an effort to reach out to students who are at-risk academically or socially and get to know them and build stronger relationships with them. Offer support to teachers in the form of an expert (counsellor or psychologist) available to staff for consultation about student issues beyond their expertise.

Models

It must be acknowledged that when considering reform, schools need to take into consideration that effective reform is evidence-based and holistic (Edwards, 2015). Therefore, to increase school connectedness, school leaders should be looking at models that have a strong research base and address students' academic, social and emotional needs. Osher et al. (2010) recognised this need, and thus surveyed three approaches to improving school discipline practices and student behaviour: ecological approaches to classroom management, school-wide positive behavioural supports (SWPBS) and social and emotional learning (SEL).

Ecological approach

An ecological approach is an indirect approach that focuses on improving the efficacy and motivational powers of classroom activities. This approach is based on the action within a classroom rather than its structure, and views the teacher's main task as gaining and maintaining student attention and cooperation by dividing the class into activity segments and getting students to participate. It is a collaborative approach, as the teacher and students create classroom order together. The emphasis of this approach is on cooperation, engagement, and motivation, rather than compliance, control and coercion. In this approach, school discipline is managed by increasing the strength and quality of classroom activities. The limitations of this approach are: (a) student resistance to participate in classroom activities, (b) inclusion in preservice teacher training, but not used as a school-wide intervention, (c) research into the ecological approach is typically qualitative, so there is no real evidence to support its efficacy, and (d) will only work when the school climate is already positive, and students receive support to succeed. However, because engaging instruction has been shown to contribute to successful classroom management, this approach shows promise as a supplement to existing approaches by promoting engagement (Osher et al., 2010).

The Health Promoting School Model (HPS) is modelled on an ecological view, and takes into account relationships and connections among groups in the school community (Rowe & Stewart, 2009). The HPS model focuses on a combination of: curriculum, teaching, learning, school policies, procedures, organisation, physical and social environment, and links with the community (health services, community agencies). The HPS model is effective in promoting connectedness in the areas of trust and safety, perceptions of being valued and relationships among staff. The model includes the following whole school and classroom-wide structural and process-based components:

Whole school level – Structural

- Policies and organisational structures to prevent bullying
- Peer support programs
- Extra curricular activities
- Support for school staff
- Fair discipline system
- Welcoming environment
- Significance of school–community partnership structures

Whole school level – Processes

- Significance of school–community partnerships
- school–home partnerships
- School partnerships with staff
- Staff-parent partnerships
- Whole-school community activity: students and family have a say in activities

Classroom level – Structural

- Significance of class organisation activities
- Importance of class-community partnerships

Classroom level – Processes

- Significance of processes of working together: student centred approach, students and teachers working together, students working with students, cooperative learning activities
- Significance of class-community partnerships: collaborative curriculum planning; joint coordination of a school project by two classes

Rowe and Stewart (2009) found that whole-school community activities are crucial, as they develop interaction across all levels of the school community. Social, celebratory activities that got students involved in the school environment were especially helpful in promoting school connectedness. Whole-school community activities encouraged links between classes, to school staff and partnerships with parents and communities. Team teaching helps to promote relationships between teachers. School strategies that were found to prevent bullying were peer support programs, extra curricular activities, support structures for staff and a fair and consistent discipline system.

School-wide positive behaviour support (SWPBS)

SWPBS is a school-wide system to teach and communicate rules. It involves rewarding students for following the rules and conducting functional behavioural assessments to design function-based interventions. This approach involves setting a small number of positively stated rules and expectations, teaching appropriate behaviour, monitoring compliance of rules, consistently enforcing rule violations with mild logical consequences and providing positive reinforcement for appropriate behaviour. This approach has a strong research base, but is teacher, not student, centred (Osher et al, 2010).

Social emotional learning (SEL)

This approach builds on the connectedness of staff, and incorporates teaching and learning that emphasise self-awareness, self-management, social awareness, relationship skills and decision-making. The premise is that this will enhance social behaviours and result in fewer conduct issues and improved academic performance. SEL evolved from research on prevention and resilience. Community agencies are seen as equal partners in the service delivery model, and there is an emphasis on understanding how economic, social and cultural factors affect a student's sense of well-being and school connectedness (Sulkowski, Demaray & Lazarus, 2016).

Common features of SEL include: (a) curriculum lessons to teach social skills and foster social, emotional and moral development, (b) generalisation is built in through home-school activities and (c) students are provided with opportunities to practise the skills they are learning. SEL is an authoritative student-focused approach with an emphasis on teacher–student relationships and student responsibility rather than reward and punishment. This approach has a strong research base to support its effectiveness. Studies have found that school-wide SEL programs improved social-emotional functioning, student attitudes towards school, behaviour, caring student–teacher relationships, peer bonding, collaborative learning. Effective at all levels of education, SEL can be implemented with integrity by teachers and other school staff without outside help (Sulkowski, Demaray & Lazarus, 2016). Programs such as: PATHS, Second Step, Steps to Respect and Caring School Communities (formally the Child Development Project) are grounded in SEL, and have been shown to reduce aggression and misbehaviour, increase socially competent behaviour and reduce bullying and arguing (Osher et al., 2010).

Osher et al. (2010) found that both SWPBS and SEL have ecological components and emphasise the prevention of misbehaviour and the promotion of behavioural and social competence, and emphasise positive techniques. Because of their differences, and the fact that each has only modest intervention effects by themselves, the authors suggest that combining SWPBS and SEL will more effectively address the various causes of student misbehaviour, and that combining the two approaches should enhance the power of each.

Children's Communities

Children's Communities is a UK model based on the *Harlem Children's Zone* and *Promise Neighbourhoods* programs from the USA (Dyson, Kerr & Wellings, 2015). This model was designed for children with low socio-economic status, and it has a strong evidence base when used with this group. The basic tenet of this model is that in order to improve outcomes for this population, two things must be accomplished: the complex lives of children must be examined in order to pinpoint factors that contribute to poor outcomes, and schools must develop responses to these factors to engage better with students, thereby improving these outcomes. The model embraces a holistic approach to intervention, as it works from birth to adulthood across all outcomes (education, health, mental health, vocational). Because changes in government in any country will affect funding and where decisions are made, and thus may impact previous gains made in this area, the model endorses the development of a long-term joint strategy with logical partners; each partner acts as its own entity, so they can be autonomous. The partners and the interventions are coordinated to enable students to move between services, and this lessens the chance that failures in some parts of the student's life will sabotage successes in others. Overall, the model is a multisystemic approach to intervention, very close to the idea of wraparound services (Bertram, Suter, Bruns & O'Rourke, 2010).

Programs

There are a number of programs in existence that claim to foster positive relationships in school, increase student engagement, and/or improve school climate.

The programs described below are by no means exhaustive; they are rather a sampling of the evidence-based programs currently available. Although many of these were developed in the U.S., they have been implemented internationally.

The Caring School Community (CSC) program

The Caring School Community (CSC) program (Center for the Collaborative Classroom, n.d.) is a nationally recognised, U.S. research-based program for grades K–6 that builds classroom and school-wide community, while developing students' social and emotional (SEL) skills and competencies. It evolved from an earlier program, the Child Development Project (CDP) (Battistich, Schaps & Wilson, 2004). The CDP incorporated aspects of classroom change (e.g., collaborative focus, teacher training in classroom management) and school-wide strategies (e.g., strengthening school community and parent education) and demonstrated important changes in students' connectedness, including their sense of the school as a community, their liking of school and their overall engagement.

Like its predecessor, CSC strengthens students' connectedness to school – an important element for increasing academic motivation and achievement and for reducing violence and delinquency. Strategies such as class meetings, a cross-age buddies program, home activities and school-wide community-building activities have been added to the CSC to help students develop respect for each other and take ownership for their learning and behaviour. The program's features aim to build relationships among students, address problematic playground behaviours and set classroom norms.

Gatehouse project

Gatehouse project was established in Australia in 1995, and has produced a framework that is a practical and flexible whole-school strategy that can be adapted for individual school and systems contexts (Glover, Patton, Butler, Di Pietro, Begg & Cahir, 2002). It includes both individual and environmentally focused components and is designed to support schools to make changes in social and learning environments, introduce important skills to the curriculum, and strengthen links between schools and communities. The framework includes guidelines to support schools in evaluating themselves and planning school-wide strategies that reduce risk factors and promote protective factors that affect student health and academic outcomes. Three components are available:

1. Team Guidelines for Whole School Change: a five-stage process to examine policies, programs and practices in school, and evaluate and address any issues.
2. Teaching resources: strategies for teaching and learning to develop positive classroom climates, and assist students with social and emotional issues.
3. Adolescent Health Survey: provide schools with student perceptions of their social and learning environments.

The school-wide program provides schools with conceptual and operational frameworks to enhance understanding of the health needs of adolescents. It aims to enhance young people's sense of connectedness to their school. The main principle of the program is that connectedness can be developed by providing young people with security, communication and positive regard. This is done by: (a) identifying risk and protective factors that are common, modifiable, under the school's influence and have strong evidence that they influence school connectedness, (b) creating an operational framework for implementation through classroom, whole school, and community partnerships and (c) use feasible evidence-based practices. The program's instructions for implementation comprise five steps:

1. Establishment: form an adolescent health team, raise awareness of issues, involve the whole school community.
2. Review: examine current policies, programs and practices and identify priorities for action.
3. Planning: plan implementation of EBPs to enhance security, communication and positive regard.
4. Training & Implementation: training and ongoing support for teachers and other staff then implement strategies.
5. Evaluation: monitor, evaluate and communicate progress, and celebrate achievements.

The program guidelines contain resources to assist with the five steps above, along with research to back up practices and make the research to practice connection for teachers.

MindMatters

MindMatters is a national mental health initiative for secondary schools developed by *beyondblue* with funding from the Australian Government Department of Health. "It is a framework that provides structure, guidance, and support while enabling schools to build their own mental health strategy to suit their unique circumstances" (MindMatters, 2014). The MindMatters program consists of blended professional learning for school staff that includes online resources, face-to-face training, webinars and support. The program has four key components: positive school community, student skills for resilience, parents and families, and support for students experiencing mental health difficulties. All of the content within the program has a strong evidence base, and the content of the program is based on the DASH-CDC's (2009) recommended strategies to increase school connectedness.

Conclusion

Although the importance of school connectedness is widely recognised and understood, how to promote connectedness is not. The evolving literature on the subject suggests that rather than piecemeal strategies, a whole school approach may be the most effective way to foster school connectedness (Rowe & Stewart, 2009). It is evident from the literature and evidence-based strategies and programs that fostering school connectedness is a group effort, involving school leaders, teachers and other school staff, students, families and the community. Although there is a dearth of research examining the school connectedness of students with disabilities specifically, the evidence base built to support strategies and programs that increase students' sense of connectedness to their school most likely had students with disabilities in their participant populations. More research is needed to evaluate the effectiveness of these strategies on the school connectedness of students with disabilities.

In order to close the research to practice gap in the area of school connectedness, school communities need to know what evidence-based programs currently exist, so they may choose programs that fit best in their specific context. They also need to ensure that whatever program they choose is properly implemented, effectively evaluated, and has a plan for continuity (Durlak, Weissberg, Dymnicki, Taylor & Schellinger, 2011). Analysing the cost effectiveness of different programs may help to increase buy-in by policy makers, legislators, and school leaders. More research is needed in the area of strategies to promote school connection among students with disabilities and other disenfranchised groups. Lastly, researching the effect of student connectedness on teacher morale, connectedness and turnover would provide a fuller picture of the benefits of fostering school connectedness.

THEORY TO PRACTICE

Suggestions can be divided into four areas:
Teacher educators can...

- Provide preservice teachers and school leaders with information about the theories supporting school connectedness interventions, and stress the link from research to practice
- Deliver instruction that provides preservice teachers with deep content knowledge, along with a range of teaching methods, and understanding about children and adolescents and how they learn
- Offer preservice teachers and school leaders the opportunity to learn about the evidence-based programs currently available to increase students' sense of connectedness to their schools
- Provide preservice teachers with knowledge on how to work with diverse groups of students
- Deliver instruction to preservice teachers and school leaders that stresses the importance of student self-determination instruction and giving students and families a voice

School leaders can...

- Be willing to incorporate well-being into the curriculum, and prioritise the use of evidence-based practices to support a diverse population of students academically, socially, emotionally and behaviourally
- Create a supportive administration that does not allow students to fail and does everything possible to retain students
- Contact students' families for positive achievements as well as for problems, and follow up when students are absent from school
- Avoid separating students into vocational and tertiary tracks, allowing all students to participate in the same curriculum and have the same high academic standards set for them
- Create multidisciplinary groups for teachers to work together and work with students in the same group
- Ensure that every student has an adult mentor or advisor
- Collaborate with teachers, school staff, students, families and community members to make positive changes in their school climate
- Provide professional development for teachers in areas related to curriculum, classroom management and school connectedness initiatives
- Provide flexible learning opportunities for parents that will support them in their parenting and allow them to be more involved in the school and their children's education

Teachers can...

- Encourage students to be involved in community service projects and service learning
- Establish high academic expectations- continuously reinforce high standards
- Use a variety of instructional methods and technology
- Differentiate instruction to ensure that the material is appropriately challenging for students with diverse abilities
- Support students who are having difficulty keeping or catching up
- Provide students with critical thinking tasks that are aligned with their interests and abilities
- Provide consistent classroom management with clear rules and consequences
- Create democratic classrooms where every student has a classroom job on a rotating basis, an equal chance to be called on and the opportunity to plan curriculum or choose assignments
- Foster caring and supportive relationships with their students
- Be a mentor or advisor to students

Policymakers can...

- Develop state and local policies that encourage the use of evidence-based practice
- Recognise the importance of preventative school programs, such as those that foster connectedness
- Create policies that support the use of school-wide school connectedness interventions
- Ensure that schools have the resources to implement evidence-based intervention programs to promote school connectedness
- Policy makers should revise policies to facilitate the ability of schools to coordinate with social and health services to facilitate student access to needed services

10

CONCLUSION

School connectedness has been defined here as the extent to which a student feels that adults and peers whom are present in their academic environment care about them as individuals, their academic success, and their overall well-being (DASH-CDC, 2009). Fostering school connectedness is a preventative approach that holistically addresses issues related to the school-to-prison pipeline, school retention, academic achievement, bullying and engagement in health-risk behaviour (Blum & Libbey, 2004; Shippen et al., 2012).

This book examined the individual domains of connectedness suggested by Libbey (2004): school bonding, school attachment, school engagement and school climate and their alignment with relation to the four components of school connectedness outlined by the DASH-CDC (2009): adult support, positive peer relationships, commitment to education and environment. Although scholars in the field of school connectedness have not thus far come to consensus on a definition of school connectedness, most agree on the domains and components listed above, as well as interventions.

The link between school climate and school connectedness is interesting, as they are considered to be domains of each other, depending on which discipline's literature is being studied. There is no denying the importance and influence of school climate on school connectedness, as it consists of safety, relationships, academic outcomes and supports, the school's physical environment and relationships. The frameworks and research presented in Chapter 3 highlight that relationship building is the greatest factor of school climate improvement, along with the suggestion that building relationships is made more prominent in teaching certification programmes. The current movements in the USA, UK and Australia to promote the importance of school climate, along with the development and continued existence of the *National School Climate Center* in the USA hold the promise of an agreement on the definition and importance of school connectedness and school climate and hopefully policies that will translate to best practice.

Students with disabilities may be the most vulnerable group of young people in regard to low levels of school connectedness, as many experience gaps in their social and emotional development that can affect their ability to effectively navigate the school environment (Chapman et al., 2013; Durlak, et al., 2011; Gresham, 2002), particularly in the areas of pro-social and school-related behaviours. The foremost issue to consider when discussing the school connectedness of students with disabilities is that very little research has been conducted that specifically targets the school connectedness of that population. The available related research includes studies in the areas of young people with disabilities and: relationships, resiliency, quality of life, inclusion, challenging behaviour at school, social contexts, teacher perceptions, mental health, risk and protective factors and belonging (Al-Yagon, 2016; Blacher et al., 2009; Burgess, 2014; Danforth, & Naraian, 2015; Gilmore et al., 2013; Gutshall, 2013; Svetaz et al., 2000). The school connectedness of students with disabilities must therefore be examined using the following suppositions: (a) due to the prevalence rates of students with disabilities in mainstream education (5–10% of the population), existing studies on school connectedness included students with disabilities in their participant pools, (b) evidence based practices for students with disabilities can be combined under the different domains of school connectedness to improve the school experiences of this population and (c) drawing attention to the lack of research in this area will encourage further targeted research on the school connectedness of students with disabilities.

School connectedness has been identified as one of the greatest protective factors for students with disabilities, particularly in the areas of mental illness and emotional distress (Shochet et al., 2016; Svetaz et al., 2000). The quality of relationships with peers and adults is central to a student's sense of connectedness, and therefore needs to be a focal point of intervention, as it has been identified as both a risk and protective factor for students with disabilities. Other important aspects of connectedness that typically impact students with disabilities on a greater level than their typically developing peers include classroom engagement, discipline policies and behaviour management.

The suggestions presented here for interventions to improve the sense of connectedness students with disabilities feel at school are based on the literature, and include targeting performance deficits, self-determination, self-advocacy, organisational skills, the environment, social emotional skills and adaptive behaviour. This highlights the need for a multilayered holistic approach that includes input and intervention involvement of schools, teachers, parents, the community and the students themselves. Forthcoming research in the field should consider the effects of such interventions on students with disabilities specifically, in order to tailor future interventions to meet the unique needs of that population in regard to improving their sense of school connectedness.

Before adopting a particular program or approach to improving school connectedness, it is important that schools perform a comprehensive assessment, such as one described in Chapter 4, in order to tailor the program to the school context it will be implemented in. Assessing school connectedness shifts the focus to contextual factors that can be targeted for intervention rather than focusing on individual characteristics such as academic achievement, especially since school connectedness has been found to have a significant positive impact on those student outcomes. To intervene and improve the sense of connectedness students with disabilities feel at school, risk and protective factors should also be assessed. The protective factors can then be fostered and used as strengths to ameliorate the risk factors. Interventions should therefore target the fostering of qualities such as school connectedness, resilience, family cohesiveness, self-discipline, problem solving skills and taking responsibility for one's own behaviour to counter risk factors such as substance abuse, poor relationships, early onset of sexuality, violence and mental health issues.

Because of the inseparable nature of the suggested domains and components, interventions targeting the school connectedness levels of students with disabilities must be comprehensive, as addressing only one or two of the recommended components is likely to produce a less than desirable result. A holistic and integrated approach to intervention has the potential to address students' social, emotional and academic needs as well as create safe learning environments (McLaughlin & Clarke, 2010; Menzies et al., 2009). Programs that promote school connectedness should involve students and families, be culturally responsive and integrate the community into the school (Anderson-Butcher, 2010; O'Brennan et al., 2014; Toshalis, 2015). Chapter 9 provided an in-depth look at each of these different types of interventions, the research that supports their use, and their effective implementation.

The concept of school connectedness was developed over time and through research and practice in various fields, most notably education, psychology and adolescent health. These disciplines can further knowledge and innovation in this area considerably by collaborating to come to consensus on a definition, domains, interventions and areas for further research. Educational scholars have begun this process with the *Wingspread Declaration on School Connections* (Blum, 2005a), but the initial meeting and resulting document are now over a decade old. A consortium of experts in school connectedness form each of the involved fields could update the synthesis of core principles of school connectedness by conducting an updated and detailed review of research on school engagement and connectedness. This newfound information could then be used to create a framework to guide schools and other stakeholders in working together to improve school bonding, school attachment, school engagement and school climate.

Throughout this book, we have tried to highlight some of the complexities related to school connectedness of students with disabilities. Although students with disabilities are generally included with their peers in school, they may face some specific challenges that could negatively affect their level of connectedness with their schools. The focus of this book has been to emphasise importance of school connectedness for students with disabilities, discuss evidence-based approaches through which this sense of connectedness can be fostered, and highlight the need for further research in the area. School connectedness is examined here through a lens of practicality, in an attempt to breach the research to practice gap. To assist in this endeavour, advice for policymakers, school leaders, teachers and other stakeholders is provided at the end of applicable chapters. It is our hope that we have succeeded in reaching our goal, and the strategies described here are both practical and effective and generate discussion and further research in the area.

REFERENCES

Adelman, H. S., & Taylor, L. (2011). Expanding school improvement policy to better address barriers to learning. *Policy Futures In Education*, 9, 431–436. http://smhp.psych.ucla.edu/pdfdocs/expandingsip.pdf

Ainsworth, M. D. S. (1979). Infant-mother attachment. *American Psychologist*, 34, 932–937.

Ainsworth, M. D., & Bowlby, J. (1991). An ethological approach to personality development. *American Psychologist*, 46, 333–341.

Alberto, P. A., & Troutman, A. C. (2013). *Applied behavior analysis for teachers* (9th ed.). Upper Saddle River, NJ: Pearson Education Inc.

Allensworth, E., & Easton, J. Q. (2007). *What matters for staying on-track and graduating in Chicago public schools*. Chicago, IL: University of Chicago Consortium on Chicago School Research.

Alliance for the Study of School Climate. (2016). *School climate assessment instruments – SCAI*. http://web.calstatela.edu/centers/schoolclimate/assessment/

Alston, R. J., Harley, D., & Lenhoff, K. (1995). Hirschi's social control theory: A sociological perspective on drug abuse among persons with disabilities. *Journal of Rehabilitation*, 31–35.

Al-Yagon, M. (2016). Perceived close relationships with parents, teachers, and peers: Predictors of social, emotional, and behavioral features in adolescents with LD or comorbid LD and ADHD. *Journal of Learning Disabilities*, 49(6), 597–615.

American Academy of Pediatrics, Council on Children with Disabilities. (2005). Care coordination in the medical home: Integrating health and related systems of care for children with special health care needs. *Pediatrics*, 116, 1238–1244.

American Psychiatric Association. (2013). *Diagnostic and statistical manual of mental disorders* (5th ed.). Arlington, VA: American Psychiatric Publishing.

Anderson, A. R., Christenson, S. L., Sinclair, M. F., & Lehr, C. A. (2004). Check & Connect: The importance of relationships for promoting engagement with school. *Journal of School Psychology*, 42, 95–113.

Anderson-Butcher, D. (2010). The promise of afterschool programs for promoting school connectedness. *The Prevention Researcher*, 17, 11–14.

Anderson-Butcher, D., & Cash, S. J. (2010). Participation in Boys & Girls Clubs, vulnerability, and problem behaviors. *Children and Youth Services Review*, 32, 672–678.

Anderson-Butcher, D., Lawson, H. A., Iachini, A., Flaspohler, O., Bean, J., & Wade-Mdivanian, R. (2010). Emergent evidence in support of a community collaboration model for school improvement. *Children & Schools*, 32, 160–171.

Andrews, D., Fisher, S., Jenson, W., Morgan, D., Reavis, H. K., & Taylor, M. (1996). *Best practices: Behavioral and educational strategies for teachers*. Longmont, CO: Sopris West.

Appleton, J. J., Christenson, S. L., & Furlong, M. J. (2008). Student engagement with school: Critical conceptual and methodological issues of the construct. *Psychology in the Schools*, 45(5), 369–386. http://dx.doi.org/10.1002/pits.20303

Araujo, B. E. (2009). Best practices in working with linguistically diverse families. *Intervention in School and Clinic*, 45, 116–123.

Armstrong, F. D., Blumberg, M. J., & Toledano, S. R. (1999). Neurobehavioral issues in childhood cancer. *School Psychology Review*, 28(2), 194–203.

Ascher, C. (1988). Improving the school–home connection for poor and minority urban students. *The Urban Review*, 20, 109–123.

Astor, R. A., Meyer, H. A., & Pinter, R. O. (2001). Elementary and middle school students' perceptions of violence-prone school sub-contexts. *Elementary School Journal*, 101, 511–528.

Ayers, W. (2016). *Teaching with conscience in an imperfect world: An invitation*. New York: Teachers College Press.

Baer, D. M., Wolfe, M. M., & Risely, T. (1968). Some current dimensions of applied behavior analysis. *Journal of Applied Behavior Analysis*, 1, 91–97.

Baker, J. A. (1999). teacher–student interaction in urban at-risk classrooms: Differential behaviour, relationships quality, and student satisfaction with school. *The Elementary School Journal*, 100, 57–70.

Baker, J. A., Dilly, L. J., Aupperlee, J. L., & Patil, S. A. (2003). The developmental context of school satisfaction: Schools as psychologically healthy environments. *School Psychology Quarterly*, 18, 206–221.

Bandura, A. (1979). Self-referent mechanisms in social learning theory. *American Psychologist*, 34(5), 439–441.

Bandura, A. (1997). *Social learning theory*. Englewood Cliffs, NJ: Prentice Hall.

Battistich, V., Schaps, E., & Wilson, N. (2004). Effects of an elementary school intervention on students' "connectedness" to school and social adjustment during middle school. *The Journal of Primary Prevention*, 24(3), 243–262.

Bearman, P. S., & Burns, L. J. (1998). Adolescents, health, and school: Early analyses from the National Longitudinal Study of Adolescent Health. *NASSP Bulletin*, 82(601), 1–12.

Bearman, P. S., & Moody, J. (2004). Suicide and friendships among American adolescents. *American Journal of Public Health*, 94, 89–95.

Benitez, D. T., Lattimore, J., & Wehmeyer, M. L. (2005). Promoting the involvement of students with emotional and behavioral disorders in career and vocational planning and decision-making: The self-determined career development model. *Behavioral Disorders*, 30, 431–447.

Bergin, C., & Bergin, D. (2009). Attachment in the classroom. *Educational Psychology Review*, 21, 141–170.

Berliner, D. C. (1986). In pursuit of the expert pedagogue. *Educational Researcher*, 15(7), 5–13.

Berry, R. A. (2006). Teacher talk during whole-class lesson: Engagement strategies to support the verbal participation of students with learning disabilities. *Learning Disabilities Research & Practice*, 21, 211–232.

Bertelli, M., Bianco, A., Rossi, M., Scuticchio, D., & Brown, I. (2011). Relationship between individual quality of life and family quality of life for people with intellectual disability living in Italy. *Journal of Intellectual Disability Research*, 55, 1136–1150.

Bertram, R., Suter, J., Bruns, E., & O'Rourke, K. (2010). Implementation research and wraparound literature: Building a research agenda. *Journal of Child and Family Studies*, 20(6), 713–726.

Biag, M. (2014). A descriptive analysis of school connectedness: The views of school personnel. *Urban Education*, 51, 1–28.

Blacher, J., & Baker, B. L. (2007). Positive impact of intellectual disability on families. *American Journal on Mental Retardation*, 112, 330–348.

Blacher, J., Baker, B., & Eisenhower, A. (2009). student–teacher relationship stability across early school years for students with intellectual disability or typical development. *American Journal of Intellectual and Developmental Disabilities*, 114(5), 322–339.

Blue-Banning, M., Summers, J. A., Frankland, H. C., Nelson, L. L., & Beegle, G. (2004). Dimensions of family and professional partnerships: Constructive guidelines for collaboration. *Exceptional Children*, 70, 167–184.

Blue-Banning, M. J., Turnbull, A. P., & Pereira, L. (2000). Group action as a support strategy for Hispanic families: Parent and professional perspectives. *Mental Retardation*, 38, 262–275.

Blum, R. W. (2005a). A case for school connectedness. *Educational Leadership*, 62(7), 16–20.

Blum, R. W. (2005b). *School connectedness: Improving the lives of students*. Baltimore, MD: Johns Hopkins Bloomberg School of Public Health.

Blum, R. W., & Libbey, H. P. (2004). Executive summary. *Journal of School Health*, 74, 231–232.

Blum, R. W., & Mmari, K. N. (2005). *Risk and protective factors affecting adolescent reproductive health in developing countries*. Baltimore, MD: John Hopkins Bloomberg School of Public Health.

Blumenfeld, P., Modell, J., Bartko, W. T., Secada, W., Fredricks, J., Friedel, J., et al. (2005). School engagement of inner city students during middle childhood. In C. R. Cooper, C. Garcia Coll, W. T. Bartko, H. M. Davis, & C. Chatman (Eds.), *Developmental pathways through middle childhood: Rethinking diversity and contexts as resources* (pp. 145–170). Mahwah, NJ: Lawrence Erlbaum.

Blumenkrantz, D., & Tapp, J. T. (2001). Alienation and education: A model for empirical study. *The Journal of Educational Research*, 71, 104–109.

Booren, L. M., Handy, D. J., & Power, T. G. (2011). Examining perceptions of school safety strategies, school climate, and violence. *Youth Violence and Juvenile Justice*, 9, 171–187.

Booth, M. Z., & Gerard, J. M. (2014). Adolescent's stage-environment fit in middle and high school: The relationships between students' perceptions of their school and themselves. *Youth and Society*, 46, 735–755.

Bowlby, J. (1982). Attachment and loss: Retrospect and prospect. *American Journal of Orthopsychiatry*, 52, 664–678.

Bowlby, R. (2007). Babies and toddlers in non-parental daycare can avoid stress and anxiety if they develop a lasting secondary attachment bond to one carer who is consistently accessible to them. *Attachment & Human Development*, 9, 307–319.

Bowman, J. H., Krohn, M. D., Gibson, C. L., & Stogner, J. M. (2012). Investigating friendship quality: An exploration of self-control and social control theories' friendship hypotheses. *Journal of Youth and Adolescence*, 41(11), 1526–1540.

Box, J. A., & Little, D. C. (2003). Cooperative small-group instruction combined with advanced organizers and their relationship to self-concept and social studies achievement of elementary school students. *Journal of Instructional Psychology*, 30, 285–288.

Brandon, R., Higgins, K., Pierce, T., Tandy, R., & Sileo, N. (2010). An exploration of the alienation experience by African American parents from their child's educational environment. *Remedial and Special Education*, 31, 208–222.

Bretherton, I. (1990). Open communication and internal working models: Their role in the development of attachment relationships. In R. A. Thompson (Ed.), *Nebraska symposium on motivation, Vol. 36: Socioemotional development* (pp. 57–113). Lincoln, NE: University of Nebraska Press.

Brigharm, N., Morocco, C. C., Clay, K., & Zigmond, N. (2006). What makes a high school a good high school for students with disabilities. *Learning Disabilities Research & Practice*, 21, 184–190.

Bronfenbrenner, U. (1974). The origins of alienation. *Scientific American*, 231(2), 53–61.

Bronfenbrenner, U. (1979). *The ecology of human development.* Cambridge, MA: Harvard University Press.

Bronfenbrenner, U., & Morris, P. A. (2006). The bioecological model of human development. In W. Damon & R. M. Lerner (Eds.), *Handbook of child psychology: Theoretical models of human development* (pp. 993–1027). New York: John Wiley & Sons.

Brown, M. R., & Brandon, R. R. (2009). Working with culturally and linguistically diverse families: Introduction to special series. *Intervention in School and Clinic*, 45, 83–84.

Brown, R. A., & Evans, W. P. (2002). Extracurricular activity and ethnicity: Creating greater school connection among diverse student populations. *Urban Education*, 37, 41–58.

Brown, R. A., & Leigh, G. K. (2000). The school connection scale: A factor analysis. *Psychological Reports*, 87, 851–858.

Bruns, E., Walrath, C. Glass-Siegel, M., & Weist, M. D. (2004). School-based mental health services in Baltimore: Association with school climate and special education referrals. *Behavior Modification*, 28(4), 491–512.

Bryan, T., Burstein, K., & Ergul, C. (2004). The social-emotional side of learning disabilities: A science-based presentation of the state of the art. *Learning Disability Quarterly*, 27, 45–51.

Bucalos, A. B., & Lingo, A. S. (2005). What kind of mangers do adolescents really need? Helping middle and secondary teachers manage classrooms effectively. *Beyond Behavior*, 14(2), 9–14.

Burgess, J. (2014). Enhancing quality of life: Teaching children who display challenging behaviours to succeed. *International Public Health Journal*, 6(2), 133–145.

Carter, E. W., Lane, K. L., Crnobori, M., Bruhn, A. L., & Oakes, W. P. (2011). Self-determination interventions for students with and at risk for emotional and behavioral disorders: Mapping the knowledge base. *Behavioral Disorders*, 36, 100–116.

Caspe, M., Lopez, M. E., & Wolos, C. (2007). *Family involvement in elementary school children's education* (Harvard Family Research Project #2). Harvard Graduate School of Education. http://www.hfrp.org/

Catalano, R. F., Berglund, M. L., Ryan, J. A., Lonczak, H. S., & Hawkins, J. D. (2002). Positive youth development in the United States: Research findings on evaluations of positive youth development programs. *Prevention & Treatment*, 5(1), 1–111.

Catalano, R. F., Haggerty, K. P., Oesterle, S., Fleming, C. B., & Hawkins, J. D. (2004). The importance of bonding to school for healthy development: Findings from the social development research group. *Journal of School Health*, 74, 252–261.

Catalano, R. F., & Hawkins, J. D. (1996). The social development model: A theory of anti social behaviour. In J. D. Hawkins (Ed.), *Delinquency and crime: Current theories* (pp. 149–197). New York: Cambridge University Press.

Center for Social and Emotional Education. (2010). School climate research summary – January 2010. *School Climate Brief*, 1(1). http://www.schoolclimate.org

Center for the Collaborative Classroom (n.d.). *Caring school community*. https://www.colla borativeclassroom.org/caring-school–community

Chan, C. S., Rhodes, J. E., Howard, W. J., Lowe, S. R., Schwartz, S. E. O., & Herrera, C. (2013). Pathways of influence in school-based mentoring: The mediating role of parent and teacher relationships. *Journal of School Psychology*, 51, 129–142.

Chapman, R. L., Buckley, L., Sheehan, M., & Shochet, I. (2013). School-based programs for increasing connectedness and reducing risk behavior: A systematic review. *Educational Psychology Review*, 25, 95–114.

Chapman, R. L., Buckley, L., Sheehan, M. C., Shochet, I. M., & Romaniuk, M. (2011). The impact of school connectedness on violent behavior, transport risk taking behaviour, and associated injuries in adolescence. *Journal of School Psychology*, 49(4), 399–410.

Chrispeels, J., & Rivero, E. (2001). Engaging Latino families for student success: How parent education can reshape parents' sense of place in the education of their children. *Peabody Journal of Education*, 76(2), 119–169.

Christenson, S. L. (2003). The family-school partnership: An opportunity to promote the learning competence of all students. *School Psychology Quarterly*, 18, 454–482.

Christenson, S. L., Reschly, A. L., Appleton, J. J., Berman-Young, S., Spanjers, D. M., & Varro, P. (2008). Best practices in fostering student engagement. In A. Thomas & J. Grimes (Eds.), *Best practices in school psychology V*. Bethesda, MD: National Association of School Psychologists.

Chung-Do, J. J., Goebert, D. A., Hamagani, F., Chang, J. Y., & Hishinuma, E. S. (2015). Understanding the role of school connectedness and its association with violent attitudes and behaviors among an ethnically diverse sample of youth. *Journal of Interpersonal Violence*. Advance online publication. doi:10.1177/0886260515588923

Cohen, J., McCabe, E. M., Michelli, N. M., & Pickeral, T. (2009). School climate: Research, policy, practice, and teacher education. *Teachers College Record*, 111(1), 180–213.

Comer, J. P., & Haynes, N. M. (1991). Parent involvement in schools: An ecological approach. *The Elementary School Journal*, 91, 271–277.

Cooper, H., Robinson, J. C., & Patall, E. A. (2006). Does homework improve academic achievement? A synthesis of research, 1987–2003. *Review of Educational Research*, 76, 1–62.

Cooper, J. O., Heron, T. E., & Heward, W. L. (2007). *Applied behaviour analysis* (2nd ed.). Upper Saddle River, NJ: Pearson Education Inc.

Costa, A., & Kallick, B. (Eds.). (2009). *Learning and leading with habits of mind: 16 essential characteristics for success*. Alexandria, VA: Association for Supervision and Curriculum Development.

Cotton, K. (2001). *New small learning communities: Findings from recent literature*. Portland, OR: Northwest Regional Education Laboratory.

Cotton, K., & Wikelund, K. R. (1989). *Parent involvement in education*. Portland, OR: Northwest Regional Education Laboratory.

Coulston, C., & Smith, K. (2013). School climate and inclusion. In T. Dary & T. Pickeral (Eds.), *School climate practices for implementation and sustainability*. A School Climate Practice Brief, Number 1. New York: National School Climate Center.

Credé, M., & Kuncel, N. R. (2008). Study habits, skills, and attitudes: The third pillar supporting collegiate academic performance. *Perspectives on Psychological Science*, 3, 425–453.

Cronoe, R., Johnson, M. J., & Elder, G. H. (2004). Intergenerational bonding in school: The behavioural and contextual correlates of student–teacher relationships. *Sociology of Education*, 77, 60–81.

Cunningham, N. J. (2007). Level of bonding to school and perception of the school environment by bullies, victims, and bully victims. *Journal of Early Adolescence*, 27, 457–478.

Curcic, S. (2009). Inclusion in PK–12: An international perspective. *International Journal of Inclusive Education*, 13(5), 517–538.

Danforth, S., & Naraian, S. (2015). This new field of inclusive education: Beginning a dialogue on conceptual foundations. *Intellectual and Developmental Disabilities*, 53(1), 70–85. doi:10.1352/1934-9556-53.1.70

Danielsen, A., G., Samdal, O., Hetland, J., & Wold, B. (2009). School-related social support and students' perceived life satisfaction. *The Journal of Educational Research*, 102, 303–318.

DASH-CDC (Centers for Disease Control and Prevention, Division of Adolescent and School Health) (2009). *School connectedness: Strategies for increasing protective factors among youth*. Atlanta, GA: U.S. Department of Health and Human Services.

DeSantis King, A. L., Huebner, S., Suldo, S. M., & Valois, R. F. (2006). An ecological view of school satisfaction in adolescence: Linkages between social support and behavior problems. *Applied Research in Quality of Life*, 1(3–4), 279–295. doi:10.1007/s11482–11007–9021–9027

Ding, C., & Hall, A. (2007). Gender, ethnicity, and grade difference in perceptions of school experiences among adolescents. *Studies in Educational Evaluation*, 33, 159–174. doi:10.1016/j.stueduc.2007.04.00doi:4

Dong, Y., Liu, Y., & Ding, C. (2012). A psychometric evaluation of a brief school relationship questionnaire. *European Journal of Psychological Assessment*, 28(1), 19–24.

Dornbusch, S. M., Erickson, K. G., Laird, J., & Wong, C. A. (2001). The relation of family and school attachment to adolescent deviance in diverse groups and communities. *Journal of Adolescent Research*, 16(4), 396–422.

Doren, B., Murray, C., & Gau, J. M. (2014). Salient predictors of school dropout among secondary students with learning disabilities. *Learning Disabilities Research & Practice*, 29, 150–159.

Dowling, F. A. (2007). Supporting parents caring for a child with a learning disability. *Nursing Standard*, 22, 14–16.

Drummond, K. V., & Stipek, D. (2004). Low-income parents' beliefs about their role in children's academic learning. *Elementary School Journal*, 104, 197–213.

Duckworth, A. L., Grant, H., Loew, B., Oettingen, G., & Gollwitzer, P. M. (2011). Self-regulation strategies improve self-discipline in adolescents: Benefits of mental contrasting and implementation intentions. *Educational Psychology*, 31, 17–26.

Duckworth, A. L., Peterson, C., Matthews, M. D., & Kelly, D. R. (2007). Grit: Perseverance and passion for long-term goals. *Journal of Personality and Social Psychology*, 92, 1087–1101.

Dunlap, G., & Fox, L. (2007). Parent-professional partnership: A valuable context for addressing challenging behaviours. *International Journal of Disability, Development and Education*, 54, 273–285.

Dunst, C. J. (2000). Revisiting "Rethinking early intervention." *Topics in Early Childhood Special Education*, 20, 95–104.

DuPaul, G. J., Gormley, M. J., & Laracy, S. D. (2013). Comorbidity of LD and ADHD: Implications of DSM-5 for assessment and treatment. *Journal of Learning Disabilities*, 46(1), 43–51.

Durlak, J. A., & Weissberg, R. P. (2007). *The impact of after-school programs that promote personal and social skills*. Chicago, IL: Collaborative for Academic, Social, and Emotional Learning.

Durlak, J. A., Weissberg, R. P., Dymnicki, A. B., Taylor, R. D., & Schellinger, K. B. (2011). The impact of enhancing students' social and emotional learning: A meta-analysis of school-based universal interventions. *Child Development*, 82(2), 405–432.

Dyson, A., Kerr, K., & Wellings, C. (2015). Children's communities and equitable outcomes. In C. McLaughlin (Ed.), *The connected school: A design for well-being supporting children and young people in schools to flourish, thrive and achieve*. London: Pearson.

Eccles, J. S., & Wigfield, A. (2002). Motivation beliefs, values, and goals. *Annual Review of Psychology*, 53, 109–132.

Edwards, A. (2015). Interprofessional working in and around the schools. In C. McLaughlin (Ed.), *The connected school: A design for well-being supporting children and young people in schools to flourish, thrive and achieve*. London: Pearson.

Edwards, P. A. (2016). *New ways to engage parents: Strategies and tools for teachers and leaders, K–12*. New York: Teachers College Press.

Epstein, J. L. (1988). How do we improve programs for parent involvement? *Educational Horizons*, 66(2), 58–59.

Epstein, J. L. (2005). Links in a professional development chain: Preservice and inservice education for effective programs of school, family, and community partnerships. *The New Educator*, 1, 124–141.

Epstein, J. L., & Sanders, M. G. (2006). Prospects for change: Preparing educators for school, family, and community partnerships. *Peabody Journal of Education*, 81, 81–120.

Epstein, J. L., Sanders, M. G., Sheldon, S. B., Simon, B. S, Salinas, K.C., Jansorn, N. R. … Williams, K. J. (2009). *School, family, and community partnerships: Your handbook for action* (3rd ed.). Thousand Oaks, CA: Corwin Press.

Eriksson, L., Welander, J., & Granlund, M. (2007). Participation in everyday school activities for children with and without disabilities. *Journal of Developmental and Physical Disabilities*, 19, 485–502.

Evans, K. R., & Lester, J. N. (2012). Zero tolerance: Moving the conversation forward. *Intervention in School and Clinic*, 48, 108–114.

Family Strengthening Policy Center. (2007). *The parenting imperative: Investing in parents so children and youth succeed*. Washington, DC: National Human Services Assembly.

Farrington, C. A., Roderick, M., Allensworth, E., Nagaoka, J., Keyes, T. S., Johnson, D. W., & Beechum, N. O. (2012). *Teaching adolescents to become learners: The roles of non-cognitive factors in shaping school performance: A critical literature review*. Chicago, IL: University of Chicago Consortium on Chicago School Research.

Fitzpatrick, M., & Knowlton, E. (2009). Bringing evidence-based self-directed intervention practices to the trenches for students with emotional and behavioural disorders. *Preventing School Failure*, 53, 253–266.

Fredricks, J. A., Blumenfeld, P., Friedel, J., & Paris, A. (2005). School engagement. In K. A. Moore & L. H. Lippman (Eds.), *What do children need to flourish? Conceptualizing and measuring indicators of positive development* (pp. 305–321). New York: Springer. doi:10.1007/0-387-23823-9_19

Fredricks, J. A., & McColskey, W. (2012). The measurement of student engagement: A comparative analysis of various methods and student self-report instruments. In S. L. Christenson, A. L. Reschly, & C. Wylie (Eds.), *Handbook of research on student engagement* (pp. 763–782). New York: Springer. doi:10.1007/978-1-4614-2018-7_37

Freeman, R., Eber, L., Anderson, C., Irvin, L., Horner, R., Bounds, M., & Dunlap, G. (2006). Building inclusive school cultures using school-wide positive behavior support: Designing effective individual support systems for students with significant disabilities. *Research & Practice for Persons with Severe Disabilities*, 31, 4–17.

Fuchs, D., Fuchs, L. S., Mathes, P. G., & Martinez, E. A. (2002). Preliminary evidence on the social standing of students with learning disabilities in PALS and No-PALS classrooms. *Learning Disabilities Research and Practice*, 17, 205–215.

Furlong, M. J., Morrison, G. M., & Jimerson, S. R. (2004). Externalizing behaviors of aggression and violence and the school context. In R. B. Rutherford, M. M. Quinn, & S. R. Mathur (Eds.), *Handbook of research in emotional and behavioral disorders* (pp. 243–261). New York: The Guilford Press.

Furlong, M. J., Whipple, A. D., St. Jean, G., Simental, J., Soliz, A., & Punthuna, S. (2003). Multiple contexts of school engagement: Moving toward a unifying framework for educational research and practice. *The California School Psychologist*, 8, 99–113.

Gage, N., Larson, A., Sugai, G., & Chafouleas, S. (2016). Student perceptions of school climate as predictors of office referrals. *American Educational Research Journal*, 53(3), 492–515.

Gangi, T. (2010). *School climate and faculty relationships: Choosing an effective assessment measure.* Unpublished doctoral dissertation, St. John's University, New York.

Gavin, K. M., & Greenfield, D. B. (1998). A comparison of levels of involvement for parents with at-risk African American kindergarten children in classrooms with high versus low teacher encouragement. *Journal of Black Psychology*, 24, 403–417.

Gay, G. (2002). *Culturally responsive teaching theory, research, and practice.* New York: Teachers College Press.

Gilmore, L., Campbell, M., Shochet, I., & Roberts, C. (2013). Resiliency profiles of children with intellectual disabilities and their typically developing peers. *Psychology in the Schools*, 50(10), 1032–1043.

Glang, A., Ettel, D., Tyler, J., & Todis, B. (2012). Educational issues and school reentry for students with traumatic brain injury [Ch. 37]. In N. Zasler, D. Katz, R. Zafonte, D. B. Arciniegas, M. R. Bullock, & J. S. Kreutzer (Eds.), *Brain injury medicine: Principles and practice (2nd ed.).* New York: Demos Medical Publishing.

Glanville, L., & Wildhagen, T. (2007). The measurement of school engagement: Assessing dimensionality and measurement in variance across race and ethnicity. *Educational and Psychological Measurement*, 6, 1019–1041. doi:10.1177/0013164406299126

Glover, S., Patton, G., Butler, H., Di Pietro, G., Begg, B., & Cahir, S. (2002). *Promoting emotional well-being: Team guidelines for whole school change.* Victoria: Centre for Adolescent Health. http://www.mentalhealthpromotion.net/resources/gatehouse-project.pdf

Goldstein, A. P. (1988). *The prepare curriculum.* Champaign, IL: Research Press.

Goldstein, A. P., & McGinnis, E. (1984). *Skillstreaming for the elementary child.* Champaign, IL: Research Press.

Goodenow, C. (1993). The psychological sense of school membership among adolescents: Scale development and educational correlates. *Psychology in the Schools*, 30, 79–90.

Gottfredson, G. D., Gottfredson, D. C., Payne, D. A., & Gottfredson, N. C. (2005). School climate predictors of school disorder: Results from a national study of delinquency prevention in schools. *Journal of Research in Crime and Delinquency*, 42, 412–444.

Gottfredson, M., & Hirschi, T. (1990). *A general theory of crime.* Stanford, CA: Stanford University Press.

Grauer, S. (2012). *The politics of school size.* http://smallschoolscoalition.com/

Greenwood, G. E., & Hickman, C. W. (1991). Research and practice in parent involvement: Implications for teacher education. *Elementary School Journal*, 91, 279.

Gresham, F. M. (2002). Social skills assessment and instruction for students with emotional and behavioral disorders. In K. L. Lane, F. M. Gresham, & T. E. O'Shaughnessy (Eds.), *Interventions for children with or at risk for emotional and behavioral disorders* (pp. 242–258). Boston, MA: Allyn & Bacon.

Gresham, F. M., & Kern, L. (2004). Internalizing behavior problems in children and adolescents. In R. B. Rutherford, M. M. Quinn, & S. R. Mathur (Eds.), *Handbook of research in emotional and behavioral disorders* (pp. 262–281). New York: The Guilford Press.

Gresham, F. M., Sugai, G., & Horner, R. H. (2001). Interpreting outcomes of social skills training for students with high-incidence disabilities. *Exceptional Children*, 67, 331–344.

Griffith, J. (1995). An empirical examination of a model of social climate in elementary schools. *Basic & Applied Social Psychology*, 17, 97–117.

Grusec, J. E. (1992). Social learning theory and developmental psychology: The legacies of Robert Sears and Albert Bandura. *Developmental Psychology*, 28, 776–786.

Guerra, N. G., & Bradshaw, C. P. (2008). Linking the prevention of problem behaviors and positive youth development: Core competencies for positive youth development and risk prevention. *New Directions for Child and Adolescent Development*, 122, 1–17.

Guo, P., Choe, J., & Higgins-D'Alessandro, A. (2011). *Report of construct validity and internal consistency findings for the comprehensive school climate inventory*. New York: Fordham University.

Gutshall, C. A. (2013). Teacher mindsets for students with and without disabilities. *Psychology in the Schools*, 50(10), 1073–1083.

Hallinan, M. T. (2008). Teacher influences on students' attachment to school. *Sociology of Education*, 81, 271–283.

Hanson, M., & Lynch, E. (2013). *Understanding families: Supportive approaches to diversity, disability and risk*. Baltimore, MD: Paul H. Brooks.

Hawkins, J. D., Guo, J., Hill, K. G., Battin-Pearson, S., & Abbot, R. D. (2001) Long-term effects of the Seattle Social Development Intervention on school bonding trajectories. *Applied Developmental Science*, 5(4), 225–236.

Hawkins, J. D., Von Cleve, E., & Catalano, R. F. (1991). Reducing early childhood aggression: Results of a primary prevention program. *Journal of the American Academy of Child & Adolescent Psychiatry*, 30, 208–217.

Hay, I., & Winn, S. (2005). Students with Asperger's Syndrome in an inclusive secondary school environment: Teachers', parents', and students' perspectives. *Australasian Journal of Special Education*, 29, 140–154.

Hay, I., Wright, S., Watson, J., Allen, J., Beswick, K., & Cranston, N. (2016). parent–child connectedness for schooling and students' performance and aspirations: An exploratory investigation. *International Journal of Educational Research*, 77, 50–61.

Haydicky, J., Wiener, J., Badali, P., Milligan, K., & Ducharme, P. (2012). Evaluation of a mindfulness-based intervention for adolescents with learning disabilities and co-occurring ADHD and anxiety. *Mindfulness*, 3(2), 151–164.

Hazel, C., Vazirabadi, G. E., Albanes, J., & Gallagher, J. (2014). Evidence of convergent and discriminant validity of the student school engagement measure. *Psychological Assessment*, 26(3), 806–814.

Hecker, B., Young, E. L., & Caldarella, P. (2014). Teacher perspectives on behaviors of middle and junior high school students at risk for emotional and behavioral disorders. *American Secondary Education*, 42, 20–32.

Hektner, J. M., Schmidt, J. A., & Csikzentmihalyi, M. (2007). *Experience sampling method: Measuring the quality of everyday life*. Thousand Oaks, CA: Sage.

Hendrickson Lohmeier, J., & Lee, S. W. (2011) A school connectedness scale for use with adolescents. *Educational Research and Evaluation*, 17(2), 85–95. doi:10.1080/13803611.2011.597108

Heward, W. L. (2003). Ten faulty notions about teaching and learning that hinder the effectiveness of special education. *The Journal of Special Education*, 36, 186–205.

Heward, W. L. (2012) *Exceptional children: An introduction to special education* (10th ed.). Upper Saddle River, NJ: Pearson.

Hirschi, T. (1969). *Causes of delinquency*. Berkeley, CA: University of California Press.

Hobbs, N. (1978). Classification options: A conversation with Nicolas Hobbs on exceptional children. *Exceptional Children*, 44, 494–497.

Hodge, N., & Runswick-Cole, K. (2008). Problematising parent-professional partnerships in education. *Disability & Society*, 23, 637–647.

Hossfeld, B., & Taormina, G. (1998). The girls circle: Providing self-esteem support groups for adolescent girls. *Resiliency in Action*, 3(2), 17–21.

Humphrey, N., & Symes, W. (2011). Peer interaction patterns among adolescents with autistic spectrum disorders (ASDs) in mainstream school settings. *Autism*, 15(4), 397–419. doi:10.1177/1362361310387804

Jager, J., Yuen, C. X., Putnick, D. L., Hendricks, C., & Bornstein, M. H. (2015). Adolescent-peer relationships, separation and detachment from parents, and internalizing and externalizing behaviors: Linkages and interactions. *The Journal of Early Adolescence*, 35, 511–537.

Jenkins, P. A. (1997). School delinquency and the school social bond. *Journal of Research in Crime and Delinquency*, 34(3), 337–367. doi:10.1177/0022427897034003003

Jimerson, S. R., Campos, E., & Greif, J. L. (2003). Toward an understanding of definitions and measures of school engagement and related terms. *The California School Psychologist*, 8, 7–27.

Johnson, K. A. (1984). The applicability of social control theory in understanding adolescent alcohol use. *Sociological Spectrum*, 4, 275–294.

Johnson, M. K., Crosnoe, R., & Thaden, L. L. (2006). Gendered patterns in adolescents' school attachment. *Social Psychology Quarterly*, 69(3), 284–295.

Jones, S. M., Brown, J. L., Hoglund, W. L. G., & Aber, J. L. (2010). A school-randomized clinical trial of an integrated social-emotional learning and literacy intervention: Impacts after 1 school year. *Journal of Consulting and Clinical Psychology*, 78(6), 829–842.

Jordan, C., Orozco, E., & Averett, A. (2002). *Emerging issues in school, family, and community connections*. Austin, TX: Southwest Educational Development Laboratory.

Kaplan Toren, N., & Seginer, R. (2015). Classroom climate, parental educational involvement, and student school functioning in early adolescence: A longitudinal study. *Social Psychology of Education*, 18, 811–827.

Kauffman, J. M., & Landrum, T. L. (2013). *Characteristics of emotional and behavioral disorders of children and youth* (10th ed.). Upper Saddle River, NJ: Pearson Education Inc.

Kavale, K. A., Mathur, S. R., & Mostert, M. P. (2004). Social skills training and teaching social behavior to students with emotional and behavior disorders. In R. B. Rutherford, M. M. Quinn, & S. R. Mathur (Eds.), *Handbook of research in emotional and behavioral disorders* (pp. 446–461). New York: The Guilford Press.

Keith, T. Z., Diamond-Hallam, C., & Fine, J. G. (2004). Longitudinal effects of in-school and out-of-school homework on high school grades. *School Psychology Quarterly*, 19, 187–211.

Kennedy, C., & Jolivette, K. (2008). The effects of positive verbal reinforcement on the time spent outside the classroom for students with emotional and behavioral disorders in a residential setting. *Behavioral Disorders*, 33, 211–221.

Kennedy, J. H., & Kennedy, C. E. (2004). Attachment theory: Implications for school psychology. *Psychology in the School*, 41, 247–259.

Kenny, K., & McGilloway, S. (2007). Caring for children with learning disabilities: An exploratory study of parental strain and coping. *British Journal of Learning Disabilities*, 35, 221–228.

Kern, L. (2015). Addressing the needs of students with social, emotional, and behavioral problems: Reflections and visions. *Remedial and Special Education*, 36, 24–27.

Kim, D. H., & Kim, J. H. (2013). Social relations and school life satisfaction in South Korea. *Social Indicator Research*, 112, 105–127. doi:10.1007/s11205–11012–0042–0048

Klem, A. M., & Connell, J. P. (2004). Relationships matter: Linking teacher support to student engagement and achievement. *Journal of School Health*, 74, 262–273.

Knopf, H. T., & Swick, K. J. (2008). Using our understanding of families to strengthen family involvement. *Early Childhood Education Journal*, 35, 419–427.

Kohl, D., Recchia, S., & Steffgen, G. (2013). Measuring school climate: An overview of measurement scales. *Educational Research*, 55(4), 411–426. doi:10.1080/00131881.2013.844944

Koonce, D. A., & Harper, W. (2005). Engaging African American parents in the schools: A community-based consultation model. *Journal of Educational and Psychological Consultation*, 16, 55–74.

Kroth, R. L., & Edge, D. (2007). *Communicating with parents and families of exceptional children.* Denver, CO: Love Publishing.

Kreider, H., Caspe, M., Kennedy, S., & Weiss, H. (2007). *Family involvement in middle and high school students' education* (Harvard Family Research Project #3). Harvard Graduate School of Education. http://www.hfrp.org/

Ladson-Billings, G. (1994). *The dreamkeepers.* San Francisco, CA: Jossey-Bass Publishing Co.

L'Engle, K. L., & Jackson, C. (2008). Socialization influences on early adolescents' cognitive susceptibility and transition to sexual intercourse. *Journal of Research on Adolescence*, 18, 353–378.

Lane, K. L., Carter, E. W., Pierson, M. R., & Glaeser, B. C. (2006). Academic, social, and behavioral characteristics of high school students with emotional disturbances or learning disabilities. *Journal of Emotional and Behavioral Disorders*, 14, 108–117.

Lareau, A. (2003). *Unequal childhoods: Class, race, and family life.* Berkeley, CA: University of California Press.

Learning First Alliance. (2001). *Every child learning: Safe and supportive school.* Washington, DC: Author.

Libbey, H. P. (2004). Measuring student relationships to school: Attachment, bonding, connectedness, and engagement. *Journal of School Health*, 74, 274–283.

Little, J. W. (1999). Organizing schools for teacher learning. In L. Darling-Hammond & G. Sykes (Eds.), *Teaching as the learning profession: Handbook of policy and practice* (pp. 233–262). San Francisco, CA: Jossey-Bass.

Lopez, V., Clifford, T., Minnes, P., & Ouellette-Kuntz, H. (2008). Parental stress and coping in families of children with and without developmental delays. *Journal on Developmental Disabilities*, 14, 99–104.

Loukas, A., Cance, J. D., & Batanova, M. (2013). Trajectories of school connectedness across the middle school years: Examining the roles of adolescents' internalizing and externalizing problems. *Youth and Society*, 48, 557–576.

Loukas, A., Suzuki, R., & Horton, K. D. (2006). Examining school connectedness as a mediator of school climate effects. *Journal of Research on Adolescence*, 16, 491–502.

Lovitt, T. C. (1973). Self-management projects with children with behavioural disabilities. *Journal of Learning Disabilities*, 6, 138–154.

Lynch, E., & Hanson, M. (Eds.). (2011). *Developing cross-cultural competence: A guide for working with children and their families* (4th ed.). Baltimore, MD: Paul H. Brooks.

Maag, J. W. (2001). Rewarded by punishment: Reflections on the disuse of positive reinforcement in schools. *Exceptional Children*, 67, 173–186.

Maddox, S. J., & Prinz, R. J. (2003). School bonding in children and adolescents. *Clinical Child and Family Psychology Review*, 6(31), 31–49. doi:10.1023/A:1022214022478

Mandell, C. J., & Murray, M. M. (2005). Innovative family-centred practices in personnel preparation. *Teacher Education and Special Education*, 28(1), 74–77.

Mapp, K. L. (2003). Having their say: Parents describe why and how they are engaged in their children's learning. *The School Community Journal*, 13(1), 35–64.

Marks, H. M. (2000). Student engagement in instructional activity: Patterns, in the elementary, middle, and high school years. *American Educational Research Journal*, 37, 153–184.

Matsueda, R. L. (1988). The current state of differential association theory. *Crime & Delinquency*, 34, 277–306.

McKenna, J. (2013). The disproportionate representation of African Americans in programs for students with emotional and behavioral disorders. *Preventing School Failure*, 57, 206–211.

McLaughlin, C., & Clarke, B. (2010). Relational matters: A review of the impact of school experience on mental health in early adolescence. *Educational & Child Psychology*, 27(1), 91–103.

McLaughlin, C., & Gray, J. (2015). Adolescent well being and the relational school. In C. McLaughlin (Ed.), *The connected school: A design for well-being supporting children and young people in schools to flourish, thrive and achieve*. London: Pearson.

McNeely, C., & Falci, C. (2004). School connectedness and the transition into and out of health-risk behavior among adolescents: A comparison of social belonging and teacher support. *Journal of School Health*, 74, 284–292.

McNeely, C. A., Nonnemaker, J. M., & Blum, R. W. (2002). Promoting student connectedness to school: Evidence from the national longitudinal study of adolescent health. *Journal of School Health*, 72, 138–146.

McWilliam, R., Maxwell, K., & Sloper, K. (1999). Beyond involvement: Are elementary schools ready to be family-centred? *School Psychology Review*, 28, 378–394.

McWilliam, R. A., Tocci, L., & Harbin, G. L. (1998). Family-centred services: Service providers' discourse and behaviour. *Topics in Early Childhood Special Education*, 18, 206–221.

Menzies, H. M., Lane, K. L., & Lee, J. M. (2009). Self-monitoring strategies for use in the classroom: A promising practice to support productive behavior for students with emotional or behavioral disorders. *Beyond Behavior*, 18(2), 27–35.

Merikangas, K. R., He, J., Burstein, M., Swanson, S. A., Avenevoli, S., Cui, L., Benjet, C., Georgiades, K., & Swendsen, J. (2010). Lifetime prevalence of mental disorders in U.S. adolescents: Results from the national comorbidity study-adolescent supplement (NCS-A). *Journal of the American Academy of Child and Adolescent Psychiatry*, 49, 980–989.

Milner, H. R. (2011). Culturally relevant pedagogy in a diverse urban classroom. *The Urban Review*, 43, 66–89.

Milsom, A. (2006). Creating positive school experiences for students with disabilities. *Professional School Counseling Journal*, 10(1), 66–72.

MindMatters. (2014). *Simple steps to improving school connectedness*. https://www.mindmatters.edu.au/docs/default-source/learning-module-documents/mm-module1-4_simplesteps_v5.pdf

Mithaug, D., Wehmeyer, M., Agran, M., Martin, J., & Palmer, S. (1998). The self-determined learning model of instruction: Engaging students to solve their own learning problems. In M. L. Wehmeyer & D. J. Sands (Eds.), *Making it happen: Student involvement in educational planning, decision making, and instruction* (pp. 299–328). Baltimore, MD: Paul H. Brookes.

Monahan, K. C., Oesterle, S., & Hawkins, J. D. (2010). Predictors and consequences of school connectedness: The case from prevention. *The Prevention Researcher*, 17, 3–6.

Moody, J. S., & Bearman, P. (2001). *School attachment*. Unpublished manuscript.

Moore, D., & Nettelbeck, T. (2013). Effects of short-term disability awareness training on attitudes of adolescent schoolboys toward persons with a disability. *Intellectual and Developmental Disabilities*, 38(3), 223–231.

Morgan, J. J. (2010). Social networking websites: Teaching appropriate social competence to students with emotional and behavioral disorders. *Intervention in School and Clinic*, 45, 147–157.

Mulholland, R., & Blecker, M. (2008). Parents and special educators: Pre-service teachers' discussion points. *International Journal of Special Education*, 23(1), 48–53.

Murray, M. M., & Curran, E. M. (2008). Learning together with parents of children with disabilities: Bringing parent-professional partnership education to a new level. *Teacher Education and Special Education*, 31(1), 59–63.

Murray, C., & Greenberg, M. T. (2001). Relationships with teachers and bonds with school: Social emotional adjustment correlates for children with and without disabilities. *Psychology in the Schools*, 38, 25–41.

Murray, C., & Greenberg, M. T. (2006). Examining the importance of social contexts in the lives of children with high incidence disabilities. *Journal of Special Education*, 39(4), 220–233.

Murray, M. M., & Mandell, C. J. (2004). Evaluation of a family-centred early childhood special education preservice model by program graduates. *Topics in Early Childhood Special Education*, 24, 238–249.

National Center for Educational Statistics (NCES). (2015). Digest of education statistics. https://nces.ed.gov/pubsearch/pubsinfo.asp?pubid=20160144.

National Center on Safe Supportive Learning Environments. (2016). ED School Climate Surveys (EDSCLS). https://safesupportivelearning.ed.gov/edscls/measures

National Institute of Child Health and Human Development. (1995). The national longitudinal study of adolescent to adult health (Add Health). http://www.cpc.unc.edu/projects/addhealth.

National Research Council and the Institute of Medicine. (2004). *Engaging schools: Fostering high school students' motivation to learn.* Committee on Increasing High School Students' Engagement and Motivation to Learn. Board on Children, Youth, and Families, Division of Behavioral and Social Sciences and Education. Washington, DC: The National Academies Press.

National School Climate Center (NSCC). (n.d.). School climate. http://www.schoolclimate.org.

National School Climate Center (NSCC). (2007). The school climate challenge: Narrowing the gap between school climate research and school climate policy, practice guidelines and teacher education policy. http://www.schoolclimate.org/climate/policy.php

National School Climate Center (NSCC). (2009). National school climate standards: Benchmarks to promote effective teaching, learning and comprehensive school improvement. Center for Social and Emotional Education. http://www.schoolclimate.org/climate/documents/school-climate-standards-csee.pdf

National School Climate Center (NSCC). (2016a). Mission/Vision. http://www.schoolclimate.org/about/mission.php.

National School Climate Center (NSCC). (2016b). Comprehensive school climate inventory. http://www.schoolclimate.org/climate/practice.php.

Newman, B. M., Lohman, B. J., & Newman, P. R. (2007). Peer group membership and a sense of belonging: Their relationship to adolescent behavior problems. *Adolescence*, 42, 241–263.

Nieto, S. (2002). Profoundly multicultural questions. *Educational Leadership*, 60, 6–10.

O'Brennan, L. M., Waasdorp, T. E., & Bradshaw, C. P. (2014). Strengthening bullying prevention through school staff connectedness. *Journal of Educational Psychology*, 106, 870–880.

Office for Standards in Education, Children's Services and Skills. (2009). *Departmental Report 2008–2009.* Retrieved 21 January 2017 from https://www.gov.uk/government/organisations/ofsted.

Olmeda, R. E., & Kauffman, J. M. (2003). Sociocultural considerations in social skills training research with African American students with emotional and behavioural disorders. *Journal of Developmental and Physical Disabilities*, 15, 101–121.

Organisation for Economic Co-operation and Development (OECD). (2016). TALIS – The OECD teaching and learning international survey. https://www.oecd.org/edu/school/talis.htm.

Osher, D., Bear, G. G., Sprague, J. R., & Doyle, W. (2010). How can we improve school discipline? *Educational Researcher*, 39(1), 48–58. doi:10.3102/0013189X09357618

Osher, T. W., & Osher, D. M. (2002). The paradigm shift to true collaboration with families. *Journal of Child and Family Studies*, 11(1), 47–60.

Osterman, K. F. (2000). Students' need for belonging in the school community. *Review of Educational Research*, 70, 323–367. doi:10.3102/00346543070003323

Ou, S. (2005). Pathways of long-term effects of an early intervention program on educational attainment: Findings from the Chicago longitudinal study. *Applied Developmental Psychology*, 26, 578–611.

Ozer, E. J., Wolf, J. P., & Kong, C. (2008). Sources of perceived school connection among ethnically diverse urban adolescents. *Journal of Adolescent Research*, 23, 438–470.

Padak, N., & Rasinski, T. V. (2010). Welcoming schools: Small changes that can make a big difference. *The Reading Teacher*, 64, 294–297.

Park, J., & Turnbull, A. P. (2003). Service integration in early intervention: Determining interpersonal and structural factors for its success. *Infants & Young Children*, 16, 48–58.

Parke, R. D. (2004). Development in the family. *Annual Review of Psychology*, 55, 365–399.

Peguero, A. A., Ovink, S. M., & Ling, Y. L. (2016). Social bonding to school and educational inequality: Race/ethnicity, dropping out, and the significance of place. *Sociological Perspectives*, 59, 317–344.

Peguero, A. A., Popp, A. M., Latimore, T. L., Shekarkhar, Z., & Koo, D. J. (2011). Social control theory and school misbehavior: Examining the role of race and ethnicity. *Youth Violence and Juvenile Justice*, 9, 259–275.

Perlman, D. J. (2013). The influence of the social context on students in-class physical activity. *Journal of Teaching in Physical Education*, 32(1), 46–60.

Petrie, K. (2014). The relationship between school climate and student bullying. *TEACH Journal of Christian Education*, 8(1), 26–35.

Popp, A. M., & Peguero, A. A. (2012). School bonds and the role of school-based victimization. *Journal of Interpersonal Violence*, 27, 3366–3388.

Positive Behavioral Interventions and Supports (PBIS). (n.d.). SWPBIS for beginners. https://www.pbis.org/school/swpbis-for-beginners

Praisner, C. L. (2003). Attitudes of elementary school principals toward the inclusion of students with disabilities. *Exceptional Children*, 69(2), 135–145.

Quint, J. (2006). *Meeting five challenges of high school reform: Lessons from research on three reform models*. New York: MDRC.

Ramirez, A. Y. (2001). Parent involvement is like apple pie: A look at parental involvement in two states. *The High School Journal*, 85(1), 1–9.

Regan, K. S., & Michaud, K. M. (2011). Best practices to support student behavior. *Beyond Behavior*, 20(2), 40–47.

Reglin, L. G., King, S., Losike-Sedimo, N., & Ketterer, A. (2003). Barriers to school involvement and strategies to enhance involvement from parents at low performing urban schools. *The Journal of at Risk Issues*, 9(2), 1–7.

Reschly, A. L., & Christenson, S. L. (2006). Prediction of dropout among students with mild disabilities: A case for inclusion of student engagement variables. *Remedial and Special Education*, 27, 276–292.

Resnick, M. D., Bearman, P., Blum, R. W., Bauman, K. E., Harris, K. M., Jones, J., Tabor, T., Beuhring, R., Sieving, M., Shew, M., Ireland, L., Beringer, L., & Udry, J. R. (1997). Protecting adolescents from harm: Findings from the National Longitudinal Study of Adolescent Health. *Journal of the American Medical Association*, 278, 823–832.

Reuther, B. T. (2014). On our everyday being: Heidegger and attachment theory. *Journal of Theoretical and Philosophical Psychology*, 34, 101–115.

Richards, H. V., Brown, A. F., & Forde, T. B. (2007). Addressing diversity in schools: Culturally responsive pedagogy. *Teaching Exceptional Children*, 39, 64–68.

Rivkin, D. H. (2009). Decriminalizing students with disabilities. *New York School Law Review*, 54, 909–952.

Ross, R. (2013). School climate and equity. In T. Dary, & T. Pickeral (Eds.), *School Climate Practices for Implementation and Sustainability. A School Climate Practice Brief*, Number 1. New York: National School Climate Center.

Rowe, F., & Stewart, D. (2009). Promoting connectedness through whole-school approaches: A qualitative study. *Health Education*, 109(5), 396–413.

Ryan, R. M., & Deci, E. L. (2000). Self-determination theory and the facilitation of intrinsic motivation, social development, and well-being. *American Psychologist*, 55, 68–78. doi:10.1037/0003-066X.55.1.68

Ryan, J. B., Pierce, C. D., & Mooney, P. (2008). Evidence-based teaching strategies for students with EBD. *Beyond Behavior*, 17, 22–29.

Saggers, B., et al. (2015). *Australian autism educational needs analysis – What are the needs of schools, parents and students on the autism spectrum?* Full report. Brisbane: Cooperative Research Centre for Living with Autism.

Savitz-Romer, M., & Jager-Hyman, J. (2009). Stronger together. *Principal Leadership*, 9(8), 48–53.

Sanders, M. (1999). Improving school, family, and community partnerships in urban middle schools. *Middle School Journal*, 31(2), 35–41.

Seifert, D., & Hartnell-Young, E. (2015). An effective school improvement framework: Using the national school improvement tool. Camberwell, VIC: Australian Council for Educational Research. http://research.acer.edu.au/cgi/viewcontent.cgi?article=1022&context=tll_misc

Shaver, P. R., Collins, N. L., & Clark, C. L. (1996). Attachment styles and internal working models of self and relationship partners. In G. J. O. Fletcher & J. Fitness (Eds.), *Knowledge structures in close relationships: A social psychological approach* (pp. 25–61). Mahwah, NJ: Erlbaum.

Shaw, S., & McCabe, P. (2008). Hospital-to-school transition for children with chronic illness: Meeting the new challenges of an evolving health care system. *Psychology in the Schools*, 45(1), 74–87.

Sheldon, S. B. (2002). Parents' social networks and beliefs as predictors of parent involvement. *Elementary School Journal*, 102, 301–316.

Sheridan, S. M., & Kratochwill, T. R. (2007). *Conjoint behavioral consultation: Promoting family-school connections and interventions*. New York: Springer.

Shippen, M. E., Patterson, D., Green, K. L., & Smitherman, T. (2012). Community and school practices to reduce delinquent behavior: Intervening on the school-to-prison pipeline. *Teacher Education and Special Education*, 35, 296–308.

Shochet, I. M., Dadds, M. R., Ham, D., & Montague, R. (2006). School connectedness is an underemphasized parameter in adolescent mental health: Results of a community prediction study. *Journal of Clinical Child and Adolescent Psychology*, 35(2), 170–179.

Shochet, I. M., Saggers, B. R., Carrington, S. B., Orr, J. A., Wurfl, A. M., Duncan, B. M., & Smith, C. L. (2016). The Cooperative Research Centre for Living with Autism (Autism CRC) conceptual model to promote mental health for adolescents with ASD. *Clinical Child and Family Psychology Review*, 19(2), 94–116.

Skiba, R. J., Michael, R. S., Nardo, A. C., & Peterson, R. L. (2002). The colour of discipline: Sources of racial and gender disproportionality in school punishment. *The Urban Review*, 34, 317–342.

Skinner, E. A., Marchand, G., Furrer, C., & Kindermann, T. (2008). Engagement and disaffection in the classroom: Part of a larger motivational dynamic. *Journal of Educational Psychology*, 100(4), 765–781. doi:10.1037/a0012840

Sorenson, A. M., & Brownfield, D. (1995). Adolescent drug use and a general theory of crime: An analysis of a theoretical integration. *Canadian Journal of Criminology*, 37, 19–35.

Spooner, F., Dymond, S. K., Smith, A., & Kennedy, C. H. (2006). What we know and need to know about accessing the general curriculum for students with significant cognitive disabilities. *Research & Practice for Persons with Severe Disabilities*, 31, 277–283.

Srsic, A., & Hess Rice, E. (2012). Understanding the experience of girls with EBD in a gender-responsive support group. *Education and Treatment of Children*, 35(4), 623–646.

Stevenson, K. R. (2006). School size and its relationship to student outcomes and school climate: A review and analysis of eight South Carolina state-wide studies. National Clearinghouse for Educational Facilities. http://www.edfacilities.org/pubs/size_outcomes.pdf

Stewart, E. B. (2008). School structural characteristics, student effort, peer associations, and parental involvement: The influence of school- and individual-level factors on academic achievement. *Education and Urban Society*, 40, 179–204.

Strnadová, I., Cumming, T., & Danker, J. (2016). Transitions for students with intellectual disability and/or autism spectrum disorders: Carer and teacher perspectives. *Australasian Journal of Special Education*, 40(2), 141–156. doi:10.1017/jse.2016.2

Suldo, S. M., Frank, M. J., Chappel, A. M., Albers, M. M., & Bateman, L. P. (2014). American high school students' perceptions of determinants of life satisfaction. *Social Indicator Research*, 118, 485–514. doi:10.1007/s11205–11013–0436–0432

Sulkowski, M. L., Demaray, M. K., & Lazarus, P. J. (2016). Connecting students to schools to support their emotional well-being and academic success. *Communiqué*, 40(7). http://www.nasponline.org/publications/periodicals/communique/issues/volume-40-issue-7/connecting-students-to-schools-to-support-their-emotional-well-being-and-academic-success

Summers, J. A., Hoffman, L., Marquis, J., Turnbull, A., Poston, D., & Nelson, L. L. (2005). Measuring the quality of family-professional partnerships in special education. *Exceptional Children*, 72, 65–83.

Sutherland, E. H. (1973). The prison as a criminological laboratory. In K. Schuessler (Ed.), *Edwin H. Sutherland on analyzing crime* (pp. 247–256). Chicago, IL: University of Chicago Press.

Svavarsdottir, E. K. (2008). Connectedness, belonging and feelings about school among healthy and chronically ill Icelandic schoolchildren. *Scandinavian Journal of the Caring Sciences*, 22, 463–471.

Svetaz, M. V., Ireland, M., & Blum, R. (2000). Adolescents with learning disabilities: Risk and protective factors associated with emotional well-being: Findings from the National Longitudinal Study of Adolescent Health. *Journal of Adolescent Health*, 27, 340–348.

Target, M., Fonagy, P., & Shmueli-Goetz, Y. (2003). Attachment representations in school-age children: The development of the child attachment interview. *Journal of Child Psychotherapy*, 29, 171–186.

Thapa, A., Cohen, J., Guffey, S., & Higgins-D'Alessandro, A. (2013). A review of school climate research. *Review of Educational Research*, 83, 357–385.

The United Nations. (1989). Convention on the Rights of the Child. *Treaty Series*, 1577, 3.

Thomas, L. (2015). Design for learning: Using design principles to transform schools. In C. McLaughlin (Ed.), *The connected school: A design for well-being supporting children and young people in schools to flourish, thrive and achieve*. London: Pearson.

Tian, L., Chen, H., & Huebner, E. S. (2014). The longitudinal relationships between basic psychological needs satisfaction at school and school related subjective well-being in adolescents. *Social Indicators Research*, 119, 353–372. doi:10.1007/s11205-013-0495-4

Toshalis, E. (2015). *Make me! Understanding and engaging student resistance in school*. Cambridge, MA: Harvard Education Press.

Turnbull, A., Turnbull, R., Erwin, E. J., Soodak, L. C., & Shogren, K. A. (2014). *Families, professionals, and exceptionality* (7th ed.). Boston, MA: Pearson.

Urbano, R. C., & Hodapp, R. M. (2007). Divorce in families of children with Down syndrome: A populations-based study. *American Journal on Mental Retardation*, 112, 261–274.

U.S. Department of Education. (2010). *A blueprint for reform: The reauthorization of the Elementary and Secondary Education Act*. Washington, DC: Author.

U.S. Department of Education. (2014). *36th annual report to Congress on the implementation of the Individuals with Disabilities Education Act, 2014*. Washington, DC: Author.

U.S. Department of Education. (2015). *Student reports of bullying and cyber-bullying: Results from the 2013 School Crime Supplement to the National Crime Victimization Survey*. Washington, DC: Author. http://nces.ed.gov/pubs2015/2015056.pdf

U.S. Department of Education. (2016). *38th annual report to Congress on the implementation of the Individuals with Disabilities Education Act, 2016*. Washington, DC: Author.

U.S. Department of Health and Human Services, Center for Disease Control and Prevention. (2014). *Youth risk behavior surveillance – United States, 2013*. http://www.cdc.gov/mmwr/p review/mmwrhtml/ss6304a1.htm

van Rosmalen, L., van der Horst, F. C. P., & van der Veer, R. (2016). From secure dependency to attachment: Mary Ainsworth's integration of Blatz's security theory into Bowlby's attachment theory. *History of Psychology*, 19(1), 22–39.

Villegas, A. M., & Lucas, T. (2002). Preparing culturally responsive teachers: Re-thinking the curriculum. *Journal of Teacher Education*, 53, 20–32.

Vincent, C. G., Horner, R. H., & Sugai, G. (2002). Developing social competence for all students. *ERIC/OSEP Digest*: ED468580. Retrieved March 10, 2006, from: http://iris.peabody.vanderbilt.edu/info_briefs/eric/ericdigests/ed468580.pdf Google Scholar

Vygotsky, L. S. (1978). *Mind and society*. Cambridge, MA: MIT Press.

Wakeman, S., Karvonen, M., & Ahumada, A. (2013). Changing instruction to increase achievement for students with moderate to severe intellectual disabilities. *Teaching Exceptional Children*, 46, 6–13.

Walker, H. M., Ramsey, E., & Gresham, F. M. (2003). Heading off disruptive behavior: How early intervention can reduce defiant behaviour and win back teaching time. *American Educator*, 26, 6–45.

Walsh, D. S., Ozaeta, J., & Wright, P. M. (2010). Transference of responsibility model goals to the school environment: Exploring the impact of a coaching club program. *Physical Education and Sport Pedagogy*, 15, 15–28.

Waters, S., Cross, D., & Shaw, T. (2010). Does the nature of schools matter? An exploration of selected school ecology factors on adolescent perceptions of school connectedness. *British Journal of Educational Psychology*, 80, 381–402.

Wehmeyer, M. L., Palmer, S. B., Agran, M., Mithaug, D. E., & Martin, J. E. (2000). Promoting causal agency: The self-determined learning model. *Exceptional Children*, 66, 439–453.

Wei, H. S., & Chen, J. K. (2010). School attachment among Taiwanese adolescents: The roles of individual characteristics, peer relationships, and teacher well-being. *Social Indicators Research*, 95, 421–436.

Weiss, H., Caspe, M., & Lopez, M. E. (2006). *Family involvement in early childhood education* (Harvard Family Research Project #1). Harvard Graduate School of Education. http://www.hfrp.org/

Wenger, E., McDermott, R. A., & Snyder, W. (2002). *Cultivating communities of practice: A guide to managing knowledge*. Boston, MA: Harvard Business Press.

Westergard, E. (2013). Teacher competencies and parental cooperation. *International Journal about Parents in Education*, 7(2), 97–107.

Whiteside-Mansell, L., Weber, J., Moore, P. C., Johnson, D., Williams, E. R., Ward, W. L., Robbins, J. M., & Phillips, B. A. (2015). School bonding in early adolescence: Psychometrics of the Brief Survey of School Bonding. *Journal of Early Adolescence*, 35(2), 245–275.

Wiatrowski, M. D., Griswold, D. B., & Roberts, M. K. (1981). Social control theory and delinquency. *American Sociological Review*, 46, 525–541.

Wilkinson-Lee, A. M., Zhang, Q., Nuno, V. L., & Wilhelm, M. S. (2011). Adolescent emotional distress: The role of family obligations and school connectedness. *Journal of Youth Adolescence*, 40, 221–230.

Winton, P. J. (2000). Early childhood intervention personnel preparation: Backward mapping for future planning. *Topics in Early Childhood Special Education*, 20, 87–94.

Wiener, J., & Daniels, L. (2016). School experiences of adolescents with Attention-Deficit/Hyperactivity Disorder. *Journal of Learning Disabilities*, 49(6), 567–581.

World Health Organization (WHO). (2003). Creating an environment for emotional and social well-being: An important responsibility of a health-promoting and child-friendly school. http://www.who.int/school_youth_health/media/en/sch_childfriendly_03_v2.pdf

World Health Organization (WHO). (2004). Health topics: Risk factors. http://www.who.int/topics/risk_factors/en/

Yazzie-Mintz, E. (2007). *Voices of students on engagement: A report on the 2006 High School Survey of Student Engagement*. Bloomington, IN: Center for Evaluation & Educational Policy, Indiana University. Retrieved 1 February 2010 from: http://ceep.indiana.edu/pdf/HSSSE_2006_Report.pdf

You, S., Ritchey, K., Furlong, M., Shochet, I. M., & Boman, P. (2011) Examination of the latent structure of the psychological sense of school membership scale. *Journal of Psychoeducational Assessment*, 29(3), 225–237.

Zarrett, N., & Lerner, R. M. (2008). *Ways to promote the positive development of children and youth*. Washington, DC: Child Trends.

Zullig, K. J., Koopman, T. M., Patton, J. M., & Ubbes, V. A. (2010). School climate: Historical review, instrument development, and school assessment. *Journal of Psychoeducational Assessment*, 28(2), 139–152.

Zullig, K. J., Huebner, E. S., & Patton, J. M. (2011). Relationships among school climate domains and school satisfaction. *Psychology in the Schools*, 48, 133–145.

INDEX

 **Taylor & Francis eBooks**

Helping you to choose the right eBooks for your Library

Add Routledge titles to your library's digital collection today. Taylor and Francis ebooks contains over 50,000 titles in the Humanities, Social Sciences, Behavioural Sciences, Built Environment and Law.

Choose from a range of subject packages or create your own!

Benefits for you

» Free MARC records
» COUNTER-compliant usage statistics
» Flexible purchase and pricing options
» All titles DRM-free.

 Free Trials Available
We offer free trials to qualifying academic, corporate and government customers.

Benefits for your user

» Off-site, anytime access via Athens or referring URL
» Print or copy pages or chapters
» Full content search
» Bookmark, highlight and annotate text
» Access to thousands of pages of quality research at the click of a button.

eCollections – Choose from over 30 subject eCollections, including:

Archaeology	Language Learning
Architecture	Law
Asian Studies	Literature
Business & Management	Media & Communication
Classical Studies	Middle East Studies
Construction	Music
Creative & Media Arts	Philosophy
Criminology & Criminal Justice	Planning
Economics	Politics
Education	Psychology & Mental Health
Energy	Religion
Engineering	Security
English Language & Linguistics	Social Work
Environment & Sustainability	Sociology
Geography	Sport
Health Studies	Theatre & Performance
History	Tourism, Hospitality & Events

For more information, pricing enquiries or to order a free trial, please contact your local sales team:
www.tandfebooks.com/page/sales